Essential

Investment

OTHER ECONOMIST BOOKS

Guide to Analysing Companies
Guide to Business Modelling
Guide to Business Planning
Guide to Economic Indicators
Guide to the European Union
Guide to Financial Management
Guide to Financial Markets
Guide to Investment Strategy
Guide to Management Ideas and Gurus
Guide to Organisation Design
Guide to Project Management
Numbers Guide
Style Guide

Book of Obituaries
Brands and Branding
Business Consulting
Business Strategy
Dealing with Financial Risk
Economics
Emerging Markets
The Future of Technology
Headhunters and How to Use Them
Mapping the Markets
Successful Strategy Execution
The City

Essential Economics
Essential Negotiation
Essentials for Board Directors

For more information on these books:
www.bloomberg.com/economistbooks

Essential

Investment

Second Edition

Philip Ryland

Bloomberg Press
New York

THE ECONOMIST IN ASSOCIATION WITH PROFILE BOOKS LTD

This edition published in the United States and Canada by Bloomberg Press
Published in the U.K. by Profile Books Ltd, 2009

Printed in Canada

1 3 5 7 9 10 8 6 4 2

Library of Congress Cataloging-in-Publication Data on file

ISBN 978-1-57660-353-6

Contents

Introduction

This is one of a series of *Economist* books that bring clarity to specialist areas of business, finance and management. The introductory essay provides an overview of investment theories, stockmarket and bond market behaviour, risk and returns, and the appendices contain a wealth of data on how the markets have performed over the years. For an understanding of the basics of many aspects of investment, the following entries in the A–Z will be helpful:

ARBITRAGE
BALANCE SHEET
BEHAVIOURAL FINANCE
BETA
BLACK-SCHOLES OPTION PRICING MODEL
BOND
CAPITAL ASSET PRICING MODEL
CASHFLOW
CLOSED-END FUND
CONVERTIBLE
DERIVATIVES
DISCOUNT RATE
DIVIDEND DISCOUNT MODEL
DIVIDEND YIELD
EARNINGS
EFFICIENT MARKET HYPOTHESIS
EQUITY
FUTURES
GEOMETRIC MEAN
INCOME STATEMENT
INTERNAL RATE OF RETURN
LEVERAGE
MUTUAL FUND
OPTION
ORDINARY SHARE
PORTFOLIO THEORY
PRICE/EARNINGS RATIO
PRIVATE EQUITY
RETURN ON CAPITAL
RISK-FREE RATE OF RETURN
STANDARD DEVIATION
TECHNICAL ANALYSIS
TIME VALUE
WARRANT

Cross references are indicated in the book by words in SMALL CAPITALS.

Investment's past and future

In the summer of 2007 it simply could not get any better. It was not just because stockmarkets throughout the developed world had recovered convincingly from the shocks doled out in the first years of the 21st century after the so-called dotcom bubble had burst. As a result, for example, the FTSE All-Share index of share prices in British companies had risen 118% from the low point to which it had fallen in early 2003. It was also because lesser-known financial indices, which were supposed to point out troubles ahead – those that measured the riskiness of share and bond markets – were behaving about as placidly as was possible.

And why not? After all, the world was growing strongly and the International Monetary Fund had just upped its forecast for global growth for 2007 from 4.9% to 5.2%; inflation, by and large, remained under control; and investors of all shapes and sizes were awash with cash to invest. In other words, there was liquidity by the bucket-load. So who would imagine that the crisis, when it emerged, would begin pretty much as a conventional credit squeeze where borrowers go to the wall because they cannot get the financing they need?

That said, there was something unusual about this crisis right from the start. The borrowers that went to the wall first were banks. The institutions that controlled the flow of credit from lenders to borrowers were the very ones that were unable to get the financing they needed to conduct their own operations. This malign twist in business life was first revealed in the sudden demise of Northern Rock, a British mortgage bank that had shaken off its origins as a building society owned by its depositors and got its shares listed on the London Stock Exchange.

As it turned out, Northern Rock's errors and shortcomings

were typical of much of the developed world's banks. But Northern Rock was also growing fast – too fast. From being just a regional player in the north-east of England in the 1990s, it got itself into the position in early 2007 where it was providing almost one in five of all new residential mortgages in England and Wales, a higher proportion than any other lender. But only a small amount of the funds it needed for all these loans came from its own branch network. Instead, Northern Rock relied on what is called the wholesale money market, an informal global network of financial institutions that borrow from and lend to each other.

Securitisation surge

Furthermore, Northern Rock used this network in a way that was becoming increasingly fashionable: it raised funds for new mortgages by selling tranches of existing mortgages via a process known as "securitisation". It would arrange to have thousands of its mortgages poured into a so-called reference pool and from this pool tranches of securities would be created and sold to eager investors. Buyers were keen because tranches could be shaped to meet almost any investment need: low-risk/low-return through to high-risk/high-return and all points in between. Indeed, even the low-risk tranches, the ones with the best quality, could offer comparatively high pay-backs because their intrinsic quality meant they could be combined with debt to lever up their returns.

However, the success of securitisation proved to be its undoing. There was too much of it. At its peak in 2006, 80% of the $600 billion of sub-prime mortgages made in the United States (that is, mortgages to comparatively high-risk borrowers) were securitised. In contrast, the respective figures for 2001 were 50% of $190 billion. At about the same time, banks were lending more via securitisations than through conventional loans that they kept on their balance sheets. As the amounts raised via securitisation rose so standards fell, and, by early 2007, it was becoming clear that sub-prime loans made after 2004 were of inferior quality to those made before. This made buyers of securitised assets increasingly wary as bad debts spread throughout America's overheated housing market. Tension rose higher when, in the summer of 2007, Bear Stearns, an American investment bank, revealed that two hedge funds it ran had been all but wiped out by losses on securitised mortgage bonds where too many mortgage holders had failed to pay what was due.

So later that summer it was openly questioned whether Northern Rock would be able to raise billions from a securitisation issue that was planned for September. Yet the bank's acute need for more cash was also well known. It had raised almost £11 billion from securitisations in the first half of 2007, though nothing since May. Meanwhile, its mortgage book had continued to grow quickly, but Northern Rock had little in the way of alternative lines of credit that it could tap and – worryingly – its share price had started to fall fast.

Northern Rock cracks

Then Northern Rock's retail depositors – the people who had savings accounts with the bank – realised what the UK's central bankers and finance-industry regulators failed to grasp, or refused to acknowledge: that Northern Rock would not be able to raise further funds via a securitisation so it was effectively insolvent. As a result, they demanded their money back. In a remarkable piece of spontaneous action they formed neat, orderly queues throughout Northern Rock's branch network and staged the first run on a British bank since Victorian times. And they did not leave till the UK government had guaranteed all of the bank's deposits, by which time it was effectively nationalised – a state of affairs that was formalised early in 2008.

Where Northern Rock led, others followed – mostly in the United States – culminating in a devastating period in September and October 2008 when the US financial system was closer to a meltdown that it had probably ever been. Within the space of ten days, the US government effectively nationalised the giant mortgage-guarantee companies Fannie Mae and Freddie Mac; bailed out the biggest insurance company in the world, AIG, with an $85 billion loan; and allowed a leading investment bank, Lehman Brothers, to go to the wall – mistakenly, as it turned out. Lehman became the biggest company ever to file for bankruptcy protection in the United States. By early October the US Congress had approved a programme to spend up to $700 billion buying dud securitised assets that were clogging up the US banking system. Soon after that, the UK government announced a scheme to part-nationalise the British clearing banks.

A crisis in the banking industry soon spread to the wider economy, in response to which banking authorities throughout the developed world slashed interest rates. By early 2009 central-bank lending rates were effectively zero in the United States and just 1.5% in the UK. Not that these moves prevented the developed economies from going into recession – usually defined as two consecutive quarters of falling national income. However, the bigger question was whether recession will become depression, where falling national income is both accompanied and stimulated by falling prices in a vicious cycle. And would the depth of a depression challenge that of the Great Depression, which wrecked the US economy in the 1930s as national output fell 30% between 1929 and 1933 then, having barely recovered, a further 13% in 1937–38?

One thing that was clear, however, was that this financial crisis has changed the investment landscape – certainly by a significant amount, and possibly profoundly. The response of equity markets was to send prices plummeting so that annual returns for 2008 from almost all the world's major stockmarkets were the worst since the end of the second world war (see Appendix 2). Meanwhile, demand for government bonds – perceived as a safe haven in troubled times – grew, so that these had an outstandingly good year.

Perhaps more significantly, the effect of 2008's losses in equities – coming on top of the losses that accumulated in 2000–02 – meant that most stockmarket indices were lower in 2009 than they had been 12 years earlier. In other words, for a significant portion of a typical investor's savings span, the returns from holding equities – even after including the effect of dividends received – were minuscule.

The long view

That is not what is supposed to happen. Indeed, it is not what has happened over the course of stockmarket history. Essentially there are 93 years of decent stockmarket data to play with. The first stockmarket index, devised by Charles Dow, goes back to 1884 and his Dow Jones Industrial Average dates from 1897. But it was not till 1915, when the number of components in the index was increased to 20, that it became a useful indicator of investors' expectations and fears. Starting that year and splitting the returns from the Dow into nine consecutive ten-year periods (see Appendix 1) reveals two notable things:

- The ten years 1986–95 were the best of the lot by a wide margin. The 12.7% annual compound growth that the Dow achieved in this period cannot be bettered. Moreover, this superior growth was achieved with mill-pond smoothness rather than the turbulence that so often afflicts stockmarkets.
- Most of the other periods were still pretty good. In only two of them, 1926–35 and 1966–75, did the Dow finish lower than it started.

It is true that these results are affected by the arbitrary nature of the start date and the choice of ten-year periods. But, whichever way the cake was cut, one conclusion still holds – that investment in the stockmarket for any decently long period, say five years or more, would be highly likely to produce acceptable returns.

As further evidence, consider the following exercise: imagine that two investors each bought a parcel of shares during 1974 when the UK stockmarket had its worst year on record. Assume, also, that one investor was unlucky enough to have bought shares when the market was at its 1974 peak (that is, before it crashed) and the other luckily bought shares at the market's low point for the year. After one year the investment returns of the two would be vastly different. Using the returns of the All-Share index as a proxy, the table shows that the unlucky investor would at worst have been carrying a 59% loss (that is, measuring from the peak at which he bought shares to the trough for the following year). Meanwhile, the lucky investor would, at best (that is, measuring from trough to peak), have been running a 159% profit.

	Returns (% per year)	
Holding period (years)	*Minimum*	*Maximum*
1	–59	159
5	8	36
10	12	25
15	13	22
20	12	18

However, as the investment period lengthens two interesting things happen. First, the unlucky investor moves into profit and the profit stabilises. Whether the investment period is 10, 15 or 20 years, the annual returns remain around 12%. Second, the gap between the best possible and worst possible investment returns narrows and stabilises. The gap of 218 percentage points between the lucky and unlucky investor after one year drops to around 13 points after ten years and continues to narrow slowly. Not that the gap is inconsequential. The power of compounding means that for the 20-year holding period an 18% annual compound return generates three times as much as a 12% return. So $1,000 invested at 18% becomes $27,393, but at 12% it grows to only $9,646. It is also important to realise that 1974 was deliberately chosen as a freakish start date, but freakishly bad from the point of view of what we are trying to show here – that satisfactory investment returns are available for equity investors who are willing to bide their time.

Would that it were that simple. Now let's introduce three factors to question that pleasant conclusion. The first deals with stockmarket volatility; the second with so-called survivorship bias; and the third disputes whether investors are rewarded simply for being patient.

Stockmarket volatility

The first factor springs from a question asked in previous editions of this book. Then it was noted that on average loss-making years occur in both the UK and US equity markets at the rate of about one year in three. For example, in the 93-year history of fully authenticated US stock returns the Dow Jones Industrial Average has had 32 down years. Yet their marked absence in the period 1975–2000 – five losing years out of 25 for the Dow (and, incidentally, just three for the UK's All-Share index) – prompted the statement:

> *In the last two decades what has happened to the losing years? The answer may be that the averages are just waiting to reassert themselves.*

Statistical purists may note that averages do not reassert themselves. They are just a passive outcome of things that happen. What happened in 1975–2000 was comparatively few down years. What has happened over a much longer timescale is down years cropping up at random but far more frequently. It is reasonable to conclude that the longer-term picture offers a more realistic view of what will occur in the future.

Survivorship bias

The second factor involves what statisticians call survivorship bias. This basically means that the performance of a group is distorted if only the returns of the survivors are measured, while those that fall by the wayside are forgotten. Many stockmarket indices are perfect examples of survivorship bias. Take the FTSE 100 index of the UK's biggest companies. This index is adjusted every quarter so that those constituents whose stockmarket value has fallen to 111th or below are relegated and other – higher-ranking – candidates are brought in. Thus losing stocks are systematically excluded. If some losers fade close to oblivion, as happened to several of the technology stocks that were in the FTSE 100 during 1999–2000, their absence from the index gives it a technical boost. Put another way, if these stocks had remained index constituents, then the Footsie's performance would have been worse than it was.

Investors do not have the luxury of being able to exclude their losers from their portfolio returns. So, to take an extreme example, someone who happened to have capital invested in Russian railway stocks in 1917 would have lost the lot. Pretty much the same is true of capital invested in German bonds during the 1920s, Australian mining stocks in the early 1970s, third-world debt in the late 1980s or, indeed, internet shares in the late 1990s. Investors who had met such misfortune would probably have an entirely different perspective from that offered by the long-term returns of the major stockmarkets that had survived the slings and arrows that events had thrown their way. Even those who had put capital into Japanese equities these past 20 years would have a very different outlook from those who had invested in, say, the UK or the United States. At the start of 2009 the Japanese share market, as measured by its best-known index, the Nikkei 225, was 77% below the peak it had touched 19 years earlier. So, the fruits of half an investment lifespan in Japanese equities would have turned

$1,000 into just $230 (currency translation effects aside) – some reward.

Clearly, those who had had the bad luck or ill judgment to put capital into markets such as these would struggle to comprehend the easy assumption that, come what may, long-term future returns will at least equal those achieved by the UK and US stock-markets over the past 100 years (that is, about 8% per year after including dividends and adjusting for inflation).

Are investors rewarded for their patience ...

Besides – and this is the third factor – long-run real returns of about 8% a year have not actually been available throughout the UK and US markets. This statistic is confined to returns from equities (that is, the shares of companies that are listed on the stock exchanges). Government bonds – the other major asset class that trades on exchanges – have generated altogether poorer figures. For example, taking the period 1891–2008, in only two decades of the 12 – the 1930s and, so far, the 2000s – have inflation-adjusted returns for bonds been better than the real return for equities. Similarly, in five of the 12 decades bonds have failed to return more than the rate of inflation: 1910–19 and the four successive decades from the 1940s to 1970s. Yet bonds have one characteristic in common with equities: investors can hold them for the long term. There is no shortage of government debt, in both the UK and the United States, which is packaged into bonds that do not mature for at least another 20 years.

This has an important implication: it brings into question the idea that investors are rewarded simply for being patient; simply for taking a long-term view. Adopt that strategy for the UK and US equity markets and, despite the past ten years, the results have been good. Do the same with UK or US government bonds – not to mention Japanese equities – and the results have been pretty lousy.

... or for taking on risk?

If this means we can no longer say that investors have been rewarded for their patience alone, it also prompts the question: what have they been rewarded for? One possible answer – as capital market theory predicts – is for taking on risk.

The *Oxford English Dictionary* defines risk as the "chance or possibility of a danger, injury or loss". For investment purposes that has been translated as "the chance that the actual outcome from an investment will differ from the expected outcome", and capital market theory assumes that investors will not take up a proposition unless they feel that the likely rewards will compensate them for this chance. That is straightforward enough, but the trouble is that quantifying risk – giving it a number that can be worked into asset-pricing models – presents problems.

The theory responds by quantifying risk for investment purposes as the price volatility of the investment in question. The price of a volatile investment bounces around a lot, but that means it bounces up as well as down. However, the most widely used statistical formulae that measure risk cannot distinguish between upward moves or downward moves. All they can do is quantify the degree of movement from an average and conclude that a lot of movement, either way, equals lots of risk. So, according to the theory, investments can be extremely risky, but can end up being hugely rewarding, which is what has happened in practice.

But there is more to it than that. First, this line of thinking hints at an implication of capital market theory which remains deeply controversial – that there is no way of telling whether the market price of a security at any time is a good one or not (that is, there is no way of telling whether the long-run change from its present level will be up or down). If that is so, price volatility might as well equate to risk.

This in turn sheds light on one of the great mysteries of investment – why investors were so well rewarded for holding equities in the period 1975–2000. This mystery is bundled up within what is called "the equity risk premium". This is jargon for the excess annual returns that investors either expect to receive or actually do receive from holding risky equities rather than risk-free government bonds (risk-free, not because they are guaranteed to produce a good return but because, for anyone holding a government bond till maturity, the interest payments and repayment of principal are known in advance, so the total return is also known).

No one can quantify the risk premium in advance, though it can always be estimated. (For details of how to do this, see Equity risk premium in the A–Z.) In early 2009, the prospective risk premium was about 4.3%. This is high compared with recent years when the premium averaged around 2–2.5%, though that is consistent with the higher future returns that investors would expect to compensate for the misery of 2008's lousy returns. The important point is that the estimated risk premium is low compared with the return of over 6% a year that investors in US or UK equities received from 1975 to 2000. In other words, on the face of it investors received more than they were seeking to persuade them to hold equities. This fact sits oddly with the notion that the advanced capital markets of the UK and the United States work so efficiently that they simply do not allow investors consistently to get something for nothing; or, at least, are efficient enough to arbitrage away excess returns which were about twice what investors were expecting.

However, if we assume that equity markets are really riskier than we had thought, the achieved risk premiums do not look so odd. If we accept that truly bad things might be happening to western capitalism – that further events at least on the scale of Japan from 1990 to 2008 are entirely possible – that risk should be factored into share prices.

Put another way, even though investors have been rewarded in the past for assuming risk, this does not mean that they will be rewarded for doing so in the future. In that context, one explanation for the wonderful equity returns that were doled out in the 1980s and 1990s is prodigious amounts of good luck. The analogy is with a gambler on a fantastic winning streak. He correctly calls the outcome of wagers time after time and in the process pockets lots of money. To the gambler and his admirers it will appear that skill – assessing form, racing conditions, the odds – is guiding his hand, and truly he will attribute his success to such things, whereas in reality good luck is the major factor. Of course, the notion that good luck can play such an important role in investing – indeed, in the fortunes of nations – is not one that we accept happily. It does not sit well with our cosy idea that events spring from logical causes susceptible to rational analysis and that, implicitly, the future can be forecast by similar reasoning.

This is a depressing train of thought. It tells us that investors are not rewarded for being patient; indeed, that they are not necessarily rewarded for taking on risk but it just so happens that, in the past 30 years in particular, they have been. It also tells us that risk and reward do not go hand in hand, as so many investment textbooks say, but that there can be risk without reward. In a way this has to be so, simply because the two are opposites. There have to be risks of sufficient magnitude which, if realised, offer no hope of an ultimate reward.

Behavioural finance

Against this backdrop, what can a poor investor do? One thing is not to despair. After all, so-called experts – and that might include this writer – get confused and give bad advice. That should not be surprising. They are only human and one very human fault is frequently to give undue importance to events that spring readily to mind. Just as someone sees a crashed car overturned by the roadside and intuitively computes the likelihood of a motor accident as far greater than it really is, so investors who witnessed the stockmarket falls of 2008 give too great a weighting to the chances of a future crash in their mental calculations. It is what behavioural psychologists call the "availability heuristic" at work – a heuristic being a way people work things out for themselves. Much of the time heuristics are useful, but they can lead to systematic errors of judgment.

Behavioural psychology is increasingly used as a tool to explain the odd ways that financial markets sometimes operate. The assumption behind financial markets, according to capital market theory, is that they are powered by rational investors acting rationally. The trouble with this explanation is that financial markets throw up too many anomalies too often for it to be completely convincing. If rationality always ruled, why are there such oddities as the January effect (the propensity for share prices to do especially well in January), the weekend effect (the propensity for shares to rise on Friday and fall on Monday), the small-cap effect (the propensity for shares in small companies to post above-average returns) and a host of others? Most damaging of all for capital market theory is the suggestion that "beta" – the statistic that is used to quantify risk more than any other in capital market pricing models – has no predictive value; that is, after adjusting for other factors, shares with high betas (the risky ones that should perform) return no more than those with low betas.

One explanation may be that the human input into financial markets does matter and behavioural finance tries to explain it. For example, it warns us against our inclination to believe that the past is susceptible to easy, yet convincing, analysis. True, that is not what we want to hear. We want determinism; in other words, a view of the past that is nice and neat and packaged so that it could never have been any other way. We like events to spring from rational causes. It helps us make sense of them. In doing so, however, we forget that the past was once the present; as messy, higgledy-piggledy and inconclusive as the present always is.

Take the credit crunch, which may be the best shorthand label for the financial crisis that took hold in 2008. This is already being written about as a process of grim inevitability that began with mistaken monetary and exchange-rate policies on the part of both the United States and China in the 1990s. From these there developed vast trade imbalances – deficits in the United States, surpluses in China – that led to enormous flows of capital back into the United States. These helped keep interest rates low which, in turn, stoked a boom in lending for house purchases, which was encouraged by successive governments. Add to the mix innovative financiers, regulatory failure, irresponsible lenders and feckless borrowers and you have an explanation for the credit crunch that makes you wonder why it was not spotted and sorted out long before the edifice came crashing down.

Just as we rely too much on flawed analysis of the past, says behavioural finance, we have too much confidence in our predictions. Not just the overconfidence that is revealed in so many decisions that went spectacularly wrong – the Western Union man who rejected Alexander Graham Bell's funny invention, the Decca recording executive who rejected The Beatles in favour of Brian Poole and The Tremeloes – but the overconfidence that is revealed in experts' decision-making. Give experts an increasing amount of information and the accuracy of their predictions remains depressingly poor and constant, yet their confidence in the outcome of their predictions rises in line with the additional information. Much of the published work in this field is on psychologists and doctors. But security analysts have not been spared and they, too, fit the pattern.

Behavioural finance also highlights the irrationality that reveals itself in a host of systematic errors to which investors are prone, such as the "disposition effect" – the tendency of investors to sell their winning stocks and stick with their losers; or the "house money effect" – investors' inclination to take on increasingly risky positions when they are doing well (named after gamblers' erroneous belief that they are playing with house money when they are ahead). This inclination might not be surprising because investors consistently place too much emphasis on what has just happened. It is what makes winners gung-ho and losers so averse to risk that they reject sensible propositions. Still, if investors cannot cope with what has just happened – "prior outcomes" in behavioural jargon – they have difficulty with "prior probabilities" too (that is, statistically what is likely to happen).

This partly explains the credit crunch. In a world of low interest rates, buying securitised assets seemed like a great way to maximise yield. Loans packaged into so-called collateralised debt obligations (CDOs) appeared to combine near certainty of income with above-average yield. So, put simply, everyone started buying them. What the institutions that clamoured for CDOs – everyone from pension funds to hedge funds – failed to grasp, or simply forgot, was that if too many of them were following the same plan, too few of them would be satisfactorily hedged when prices started to fall. So, the very factors that drove the price of CDOs would also conspire to bring them down with a wallop. Everyone was in the same boat or, to use investment jargon, there was a systematic failure to diversify and too many forgot the prior probability arising from such a situation.

Understanding at least the basics of behavioural finance – and therefore being aware of investors' shortcomings – is a key building block to becoming a better investor. That is necessary because the answer to our earlier question – what is a poor investor to do? – is, quite simply, go ahead and invest, because there really is little choice. To invest in stockmarkets – either directly or indirectly – is the lot of almost anyone with surplus capital to deploy, savings to accumulate and a retirement to plan for. Certainly the investment future may not be golden; it may be downright awful. Who knows? After all, one message of this essay is that we really cannot tell. The only thing we know about the future is that one day it will be the present and, therefore, it must be planned for.

Other building blocks

Other building blocks, some of which have been mentioned and all of which are dealt with in the A–Z, are probability theory, statistical analysis, fundamental analysis, technical analysis, capital market theory and the efficient market hypothesis. Grasp these and you should have a decent foundation, but first you need to plan.

The starting point for investing often runs along this sort of line: you have a lump sum and/or a stream of surplus income and you want to turn it into something more substantial. The first step is to consider the needs for future consumption. Such questions do not have easy answers, but they can be answered approximately. For example, imagine someone decides that in 25 years' time they will need an annual investment income that is worth the inflation-adjusted equivalent of $20,000 today. How much capital will be needed to generate that amount? First, assume that inflation averages 3% a year for the next 25 years, so the inflation-adjusted income would be $\$20{,}000 \times (1.03)^{25} = \$41{,}875$. Next, assume that this income is to be paid from a lump of capital as a 6% annuity. How much capital is needed to generate such a return at 6%? The answer is almost $700,000. If our saver starts with $50,000 of capital, by what annual compound rate must that sum grow to become $700,000 by the due date? The answer is 11%. This is the compounding rate that turns $50,000 into $700,000 over 25 years. Whether achieving such a rate of return is feasible is another matter. If our investor believes that the UK's stockmarket performance over the next 25 years will be much like the last 25 then, despite the poor performance of the past ten years, it should be – just about. If, however, returns regress to something like their longer-term average, there would be a shortfall.

Granted, considerations are rarely as straightforward as this, but they move along similar lines. The key questions for investors are: what will I need and when will I need it? The answers to these will then influence the fundamental investment question:

how can I get it? It is self evident that a given money target will be easier to hit the lower the investment return needed to achieve it and the longer the time allowed to do it. From this, investment styles will flow. The lucky ones may discover that they have little need for investment. Dumping their bundle into a 25-year government bond will achieve all they need, in which case they can forget about investing and donate this book to a needy relative. Others – most others – will find that something more is needed, in which case they need these building blocks:

- **Probability theory** because, whether we care to admit it or not, investment is a form of gambling so knowing how to calculate the likelihood of certain events happening – and the price implications therein – is a vital tool.
- **Statistical analysis** because much of the language of capital market theory is written in statistics, for example mean-variance analysis, standard deviation and regression coefficients. It may not be much fun, but if you are fazed by a sigma sign, you won't understand the dividend discount model and much more.
- **Fundamental analysis** because much of equity investment is about the analysis of companies and their share prices (this is what it is shorthand for). You may dispute whether fundamental analysis is any use at all – which is perfectly acceptable – but it is difficult to judge unless you can put a value on a company's shares based on the fundamentals of the industry in which the company competes, its performance therein, its profits and capital employed.
- **Technical analysis** because, like behavioural finance, it tries to factor the human element into stockmarkets. It does this by using charts, which is demeaning for intellectuals, but charts can package a lot of information succinctly and get the thought processes moving.

- **Capital market theory** because, using a synthesis of statistical analysis and probability theory, it poses the most rigorous questions about the worth of investing. Of course you can happily spend a lifetime in investing without worrying about the likes of the capital asset pricing model, but that is not a reason to ignore it.
- **The efficient market hypothesis** because this, more than any other part of investment theory, will make you question whether it is worth the effort to try to achieve above-average returns.

Emanating from capital market theory, the efficient market hypothesis basically says that investors cannot expect to make excess returns without taking on extra risk, or being able to do something special or simply being lucky. If so, there is little point spending all those hours sweating over company analysis, accounting standards and investment techniques because the effort will bring no reward. Maybe. The efficient market hypothesis is investment's biggest conundrum. There may indeed be no more successful investors around than the laws of chance allow, and the fact that markets are efficient does not mean they cannot be volatile. But if price movements are far greater than warranted by the significance of the events that move them, and all those pricing anomalies that we mentioned earlier keep cropping up, perhaps markets are not so efficient. Besides, if they are efficient – if they only allow excess returns under very special circumstances – investment is just about the only human activity where a combination of talent and application (and, admittedly, at least a modicum of good luck) does not bring a reward.

Summary

To sum up, long-term returns from investing in shares in the United States and the UK have been good, despite the poor returns of the past ten years. It seems therefore that investors have been rewarded for being patient. However, this is not so. It is more likely that they have been rewarded for taking on risk. But the assumption that they will always be rewarded for assuming risk cannot always hold good. Such an assumption stems from focusing on stockmarkets that have survived. Yet survival is not guaranteed. There must be risks that, once realised, offer no hope of recovery. Investors who bought Japanese shares in 1990 have grasped this stark reality. Those who buy UK shares in 2009 may reach the same conclusion in 2029 – we just do not know. Despite this, in affluent nations many people have little choice but to invest in capital markets in general and equities in particular. It therefore behoves them to invest sensibly, which means with at least a modicum of knowledge. Reading this book may help that. It certainly does not guarantee the reader a reward. But, hopefully, it will be a start.

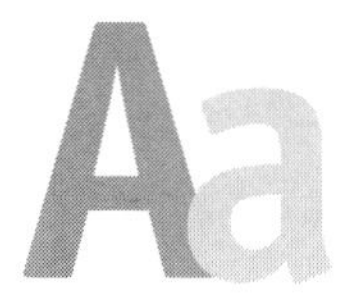

Accruals concept

A basic idea on which company accounts are based: that cause and effect should be linked by matching the costs which are incurred in running a business with the resultant revenue earned (although not necessarily received in cash) in the same accounting period. The alternative would be to have a system of cataloguing the cash transactions of a business and calling the net result profit or loss. But in any one year this would be likely to distort the picture of the company's performance since many cash costs would be incurred, or income received, in respect of pieces of work that span more than one accounting year.

Accrued interest

The interest that has been earned on a BOND since its most recent DIVIDEND was paid. The market price for bonds ignores this element; it quotes the price of bonds "clean" of accrued interest. However, a buyer would have to pay for the interest that has accrued. Imagine a bond with a 10% COUPON. If it were quoted in the market at $125 120 days after the last dividend had been paid, then, ignoring dealing costs, a buyer would have to pay $125 plus $^{120}/_{365}$ of $10; that is, $128.29.

ACT

See ADVANCE CORPORATION TAX.

ADR

See AMERICAN DEPOSITARY RECEIPT.

Advance corporation tax

A taxation system used by the UK government to take a slice of income from the DIVIDENDS that companies paid to their shareholders. However, advance corporation tax (ACT) had a penal effect on UK-based companies that made most of their profits overseas and was abolished in April 1999. Thus companies no longer have to pay the government 25% of the amount of the dividend that they paid to their shareholders. Correspondingly, shareholders no longer receive a tax credit equal to the value of the ACT paid. The exception to this rule, however, is that private investors still get a small tax credit, equal to 11% of the dividend that they receive, which they can offset against their tax LIABILITY.

Advance-decline line

Also known as the breadth of market indicator, this plots the number of share prices that rise minus the number of share prices that fall over a specific period (usually a day or a week) for a given stockmarket average (the S&P 500 INDEX, for example). Followers of TECHNICAL ANALYSIS use this to gauge the strength of a stockmarket. In particular, if the advance-decline line shows a negative return (that is, more shares fall than rise) yet the stockmarket index continues to rise, they see this as an indication that the market is weak and as a prelude to a fall in the index.

AIM

See ALTERNATIVE INVESTMENT MARKET.

All-Share Index

See FTSE ALL-SHARE INDEX.

Alpha

Alpha may or may not exist. Statistically, it certainly does. However, whether it exists in the world of investment management – as some would claim – is open to question. The importance of alpha is that statistically it can be used to quantify the extent to which a fund manager adds value to the portfolio being managed. Clearly this is significant. The more a manager can show that value has been added, the more investors will want to put their capital into the fund, and the more the manager can justify high performance fees.

Alpha is especially important for a manager of a HEDGE FUND, since the aim of such funds is to add value to their portfolio regardless of the conditions of the markets in which they operate. Statistically speaking, this means hedge funds have no interest in BETA – the extent to which returns are generated by exposure to underlying markets – but only in alpha, the return that they generate from their own efforts.

The difficulty is that the statistical measure of alpha is simply the byproduct of a least-squares regression equation that seeks to fit a straight line to show the trend in a scattering of points on a chart. So there will always be an alpha for a fund manager's performance – though it can be a minus quantity, which would imply that the manager's efforts deduct value. But it may not be significant in the sense that it has no predictive power. Indeed, the more that research is done into the performance of funds with a high alpha, the more it seems that alpha is really just the beta that is generated by other market forces. So, for example, a fund may have a high alpha when its returns are plotted against a stockmarket's returns. But the alpha – that is, the supposed added value

– may disappear if returns are plotted against another variable, say interest rates.

Note that alpha can also denote that portion of a company's share-price performance that is independent of the stockmarket in which its shares trade.

Alternative Investment Market

The LONDON STOCK EXCHANGE's junior market for small, fast-growing companies, launched in June 1995. Its progress to date has substantially exceeded expectations and at the end of September 2008, 1,608 companies were quoted on the Alternative Investment Market (AIM) with a combined stockmarket value of £45 billion. The logic behind AIM was to form a market with a minimum of regulation and spiced with tax breaks, thus creating a cheap means of raising risk capital for young companies. Since its launch, over 3,000 companies have had their shares quoted on AIM, raising over £32 billion in the process. Regulation is carried out by approved advisers rather than the exchange itself; and the information that companies have to supply is minimal as is the number of shares that have to be made available for trading.

American depositary receipt

Most US investors who own shares in foreign corporations do so via American depositary receipts (ADRS). There is nothing to stop them buying overseas shares directly (although they may technically infringe the 1933 Securities Act when they come to sell them). ADRS, however, are much more convenient. Basically, they are tradable receipts which say that the underlying shares represented by the ADRS are held on deposit by a bank in the corporation's home country. The depository bank collects dividends, pays local taxes and distributes them converted into dollars. Additionally, holders of ADRS usually have all the rights of shareholders who own their STOCK directly. The vast majority of overseas corporations that list their shares on a US exchange use ADRS; at the end of 2008 there were over 1,000 such listings. ADRS have spawned imitators and nowadays there are global depositary receipts, basically ADRS which are traded on OVER-THE-COUNTER markets in both the United States and the EUROMARKET, and European depositary receipts, which are traded on European exchanges.

American Stock Exchange

For decades the American Stock Exchange (Amex) was New York's other stockmarket, in the shadow of its bigger rival, the NEW YORK STOCK EXCHANGE (NYSE). But no longer, because in October 2008 the parent company of the NYSE – NYSE EURONEXT – bought Amex for $260m in stock. Since then, Amex has been merged into Euronext's operations for trading shares in small companies and is now called NYSE Alternext US. At the time of the takeover 1,600 issues were listed on Amex with a market value of $64 billion.

Amex's origins date back to street trading in the late 19th century and it was not until 1921 that it moved to a permanent building in Trinity Place in New York's financial district, where it is still based. By the mid-1960s the volume of stocks traded on Amex reached half that traded on the NYSE. After that, its relative importance declined. In 1998 it merged with the operators of NASDAQ, although it continued to be run independently and in 2004 its members reacquired control of the exchange.

As well as trading shares in smaller companies, Amex has been most successful in developing its DERIVATIVES trading, especially in EXCHANGE TRADED FUNDS (ETFS). It launched these in 1993 and dominates ETF trading in the United States.

Amortisation

US terminology for DEPRECIATION. In the UK amortisation generally refers to writing off the cost of INTANGIBLE ASSETS.

Annual report

All companies whose owners have a limited LIABILITY to the financial obligations of their company must publish an annual report, which is sent to the owners and lodged with a central authority for public inspection. For companies whose shares are listed on a recognised stock exchange, the annual report will almost certainly contain a mix of statutory information and information given voluntarily by the management. The statutory information includes an INCOME STATEMENT, BALANCE SHEET (statement of financial position in the United States) and CASH FLOW statement, together with explanatory notes to these.

Annuity

An annual sum paid in perpetuity, usually for a fixed amount, although it can be linked to an index.

APT

See ARBITRAGE PRICING THEORY.

Arbitrage

To arbitrage is to make a profit without RISK and, therefore, with no net exposure of capital. In practice, it requires an arbitrager simultaneously to buy and sell the same ASSET – or, more likely, two bundles of assets that amount to the same – and pocket the difference. Before financial markets were truly global, arbitraging was most readily identified with selling a currency in one financial centre and buying it more cheaply in another. The game has now moved on a little, but, for example, there would be the potential to make risk-free profits if dollar interest rates were sufficiently high to allow traders to swap their euros for dollars and be left with extra income after they had covered the cost of their currency insurance by selling dollars forward in the FUTURES market. Similarly, arbitrage opportunities can be exploited by replicating the features of a portfolio of shares through a combination of EQUITY futures and bonds then simultaneously selling the actual stocks in the market. (See RISK ARBITRAGE.)

Arbitrage pricing theory

A theory which aims to estimate returns and, by implication, the correct prices of investments. Intellectually, it is an extension of the CAPITAL ASSET PRICING MODEL. It says that the CAP-M is inadequate because it assumes that only one factor – the market – determines the price of an investment, whereas common sense tells us that several factors will have a major impact on its price in the long term. Put those factors into a model and you are making progress.

Thus arbitrage pricing theory (APT) defines expected returns on, say, an ORDINARY SHARE as the RISK-FREE RATE OF RETURN plus the sum of the share's sensitivity to various independent factors. (Here sensitivity, as with the CAP-M, is defined by the share's BETA.) The problem is to identify which factors to choose. This difficulty is compounded by academic studies which have come up with varying conclusions about the number and identity of the key factors, although benchmarks for interest rates, inflation, industrial activity and exchange rates loom large in tests.

In practice, the aim of using APT would be simultaneously to buy and sell a range of shares whose sensitivity to the chosen factors was such that a profit could be made while all exposure to the effect of the key variables and all capital outlay were cancelled out. To the extent that APT assumes that markets always seek equilibrium, it says that the market would rapidly price away such ARBITRAGE profits.

Alternatively, a portfolio could be chosen which could be expected to outperform the market if there were unexpected changes in one or more key factors used in the model, say industrial activity and interest rates. As such, however, that would be doing little more than betting on changes in industrial production and interest rates and would not have much to do with minimising RISK for a given return. Resolving problems such as these means that APT gives greater cause for thought to academics than to investors.

Arithmetic mean

The full term for what non-mathematicians intuitively call the average and which is generally shortened simply to the mean. It is calculated by taking the sum of a series of values and dividing that number by the number of values. So if 12 values add up to 96, the average is eight. It should not be confused with the GEOMETRIC MEAN, under which heading there is a fuller discussion of the circumstances in which it is more appropriate to use one or the other.

Asset

For something so fundamental to investment the surprise is that the definition of an asset is so vague. The US accounting standards body has defined it as being "probable future economic benefits obtained or controlled by a particular entity as a result of past transactions or events". However, within the context of a company's BALANCE SHEET, an asset is also a deferred cost. If a company shows plant and equipment of £1m in its balance sheet, that represents past expenditures which have yet to be written off and which, according to the ACCRUALS CONCEPT of accounting, will be depreciated as the plant is used up. The test of whether the plant is ultimately an asset or a LIABILITY will be whether it generates after-tax revenue greater than its cost. For a company to survive, most plant and equipment must pass that test. But for other items which are carried forward as assets, such as the deferred cost of a pension fund, there is no suggestion that they can bring economic benefits.

More generally, the broad categories of investments within a portfolio – shares, bonds, property – are known as assets. Hence the term ASSET ALLOCATION.

Asset allocation

The process of deciding in which sorts of assets to make investments and what proportion of total capital available should be allocated to each choice. The task is as relevant to private investors as it is to giant savings institutions. The latter formalise the process rather more, however, often beginning with a top-down approach, which decides both in which ASSET classes to make investments (shares, bonds, real estate, cash, other classes) and in which geographical areas to invest (North America, Europe, East Asia, emerging markets, for example). Estimates of the likely returns from individual investment choices compared with the target return that the institution seeks will drive the selection process. From this will follow the decision to invest an above-average or below-average proportion of funds in some markets with reference to benchmark weightings that are commercially available.

Asset stripping

A term first coined in the UK in the late 1960s to describe the practice of taking over a company, splitting it into parts and selling them for a profit. It was a derogatory label since it implied no effort on the part of the acquirer to develop the company. By the late 1980s asset stripping was more in tune with the spirit of the times, so when the practice once more swept through the corporations of the UK and the United States it was more likely to be called "financial restructuring".

> *The key to a successful portfolio is proper management of your assets and stripping should be left to wallpaper products.*
>
> Jim Slater

Backwardation

In a FUTURES market the price of a contract for future delivery of, say, a commodity usually trades above the SPOT PRICE because the notional interest received from holding cash rather than the underlying commodity is added to the cost of the contract. Sometimes, however, demand for the commodity pushes the spot price above the futures price. This is a backwardation, also known as an inverted market.

Balance sheet

The financial statement of what a company owns and what it owes at a particular date, known as the statement of financial position in the United States. Traditionally, the left-hand side of the balance sheet is a schedule of the company's assets (land, buildings, plant and equipment, cash and inventories); the right-hand side is a statement of the liabilities, either real or potential. Real liabilities comprise the debts the company must pay – that is, creditors – plus its loans. Potential liabilities are the allowances that are likely to be paid: deferred taxes and, increasingly, post-retirement benefits for employees. The remaining item on the right-hand side is the shareholders' interest in the business. This is technically not a LIABILITY at all, but a statement of the RISK capital subscribed to the business adjusted by the aggregate of retained EARNINGS and (possibly) revaluation of some assets. The following example is a potted version of a company's balance sheet.

Assets ($ billion)		*Liabilities ($ billion)*	
Properties, land, equipment	19.6	Short-term debt	2.7
Intangible assets	19.3	Long-term debt	13.1
Inventories & cash	14.9	Allowances	8.0
		Deferred taxes	3.7
		Other liabilities	12.3
		Stockholders' equity	14.0
	53.8		**53.8**

Balanced fund

A MUTUAL FUND that invests in a combination of ORDINARY SHARES and BONDS (including government debt). As such, it has a wide spread of ASSETS and could be considered medium risk, in contrast to funds that are invested wholly in equities (high risk) and wholly in bonds (low risk). The consequence of this should be that the investment return of a balanced fund will be pedestrian compared with an EQUITY fund during a BULL market, but will do well during a BEAR market.

Bar chart

A common type of price chart used to identify patterns that may give clues to future price movements in the investment under scrutiny. Price is plotted vertically and time horizontally. The price change for each unit of time – day, week, month, and so on – is plotted by a vertical bar, the top and bottom representing the high and low respectively for each period. Usually there will be a horizontal tick attached to the bar, representing the closing price. On the bottom of the chart more bars sometimes plot the volume of business transacted, scaled to the right-hand axis. This helps correlate price changes to volume of business done, which may be significant. For example, a surge in the price of a share to new

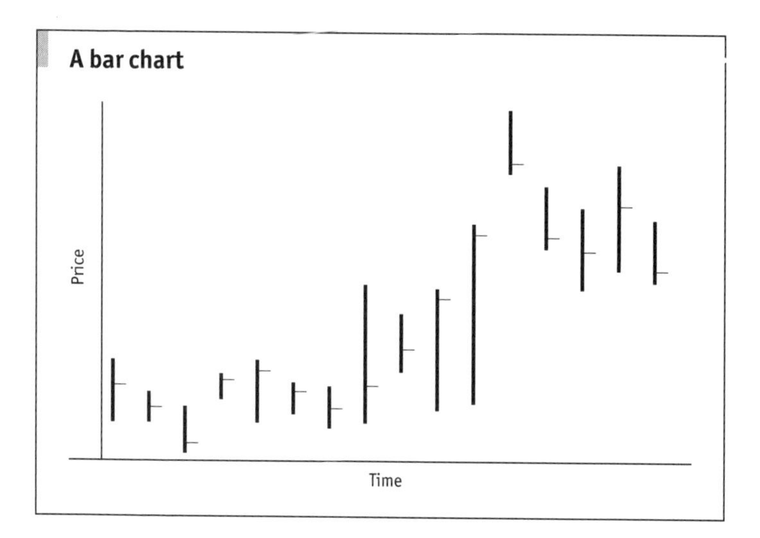

highs based on little volume could be a sign of impending weakness or, alternatively, a sign of strength if the buying has been done by informed insiders.

Bargain issue

The Holy Grail for followers of VALUE INVESTING. The term has a general meaning indicating good value in an ORDINARY SHARE. However, through the writing of Benjamin GRAHAM, it also has a specific meaning which was successfully applied by Graham and continues to be used by orthodox value investors, although usually with some modifications. These allow for the fact that stockmarkets are now generally more highly valued than when Graham was working from the 1930s to the 1970s.

The specific meaning of a bargain issue is when a company's ordinary shares sell in the market for less than the per share book value of current assets after deducting all other claims on the business. In other words, take a company's current assets (inventories, debtors, cash) and deduct not only the current liabilities (creditors, short-term borrowings) but also the long-term borrowings and any other allowances. The net result is that the shares of such companies sell for less than the value of net current assets with any fixed assets thrown in for nothing. Graham found that buying a selection of such shares across a variety of industries invariably produced good investment returns.

Basis

In a FUTURES market, basis is defined as the cash price (or SPOT PRICE) of whatever is being traded minus its futures price for the contract in question. It is important because changes in the relationship between cash and futures prices affect the value of using futures as a HEDGE. A hedge, however, will always reduce RISK as long as the VOLATILITY of the basis is less than the volatility of the price of whatever is being hedged.

Basis point

One hundredth of a percentage point. Basis points are used in currency and BOND markets where the sizes of trades mean that large amounts of money can change hands on small price movements. Thus if the YIELD on a TREASURY BILL rose from 5.25% to 5.33%, the change would have been eight basis points.

Bear

Someone who acts on the assumption that the price of a security in which he deals will fall. The origin is unknown, although it was common in London by the time of the SOUTH SEA BUBBLE (1720). It probably derives from the occupation of a bear-skin jobber, about whom the saying went: "He's sold the bear's skin before he's caught the bear."

Bear squeeze

If too many speculators simultaneously sell STOCK they do not own in the hope of buying it back more cheaply later for a profit, they risk getting caught in a bear squeeze. The dealers from whom they must eventually buy stock to settle their obligations raise prices against them. When the bears scramble for stock to limit their losses they push up prices still further.

Bearer security

A security for which evidence of ownership is provided by possession of the security's certificate. The issuer keeps no record of ownership. A EUROBOND is generally issued in bearer form. It was common for the US Treasury and municipal authorities to issue bearer bonds too. However, in order to combat money laundering this was made illegal in 1983.

“ *Invest in companies whose chairman is less than 5′8″ tall.*
Nigel Lawson, former UK chancellor of the exchequer

Behavioural finance

A fashionable field of study to explain how financial markets work. Essentially, behavioural finance tries to put people back into the equation. Much of the influential academic work of the 1950s and 1960s assumed that market prices were determined by profit-seeking individuals acting rationally. However, this work, which generated PORTFOLIO THEORY and the EFFICIENT MARKET HYPOTHESIS, could not explain many of the pricing anomalies that regularly crop up (for example, see CALENDAR EFFECT and SMALL CAP STOCK). Behavioural finance tackles these issues by applying the methods of behavioural psychology to investors' behaviour. In particular, it takes the rules of thumb that people use in everyday life to make judgments under conditions of uncertainty and examines their shortcomings from the point of view of PROBABILITY THEORY. Such rules of thumb fall into three main categories:

- **Representativeness.** People make consistently poor predictions when they think that an instance is representative of a wider category. For example, the more favourable the description of a company, the more likely it is that investment analysts will forecast good profits growth and a high price for its shares because favourable descriptions imply success. They ignore the point that a forecast does not become more accurate as the description on which it is based becomes more favourable.
- **Availability.** People draw conclusions faster and more confidently the more readily they can recall similar instances. For example, they believe that the chance of a stockmarket crash is much greater than statistically likely if there has been a recent crash that springs to mind.
- **Anchoring and adjustment.** People make predictions by adjusting an initial calculation, but too often they make insufficient adjustment. For example, when estimating the likelihood that a company can bring a new product to market, analysts are often too optimistic. They underestimate the sequence of events that must be successfully negotiated. Even if the probability of success at each stage of the process is high, the overall probability of success will be lower and will decline the more stages that have to be passed.

Bellwether stock

Just as the bellwether sheep is the one in the flock that all the others follow, so a bellwether STOCK is the one that is supposed to lead a market. It follows, therefore, that such stocks will be the ones with a big capitalisation, which can also reflect signs of which way the economies in which they trade are heading. In the UK Vodafone and BP fulfil this role as do, for example, Microsoft, General Motors and General Electric in the United States and Mitsubishi and Nippon Steel in Japan.

Beta

A widely used statistic which measures the sensitivity of the price of an investment to movements in an underlying market. In other words, beta measures an investment's price VOLATILITY, which is a substitute for its RISK. The important point is that beta is a relative, not an absolute, measure of risk. In stockmarket terms, it defines the relationship between the returns on a share and the market's returns (the most commonly used absolute measure of risk is STANDARD DEVIATION). But in so far as much of PORTFOLIO THEORY says that a share's returns will be driven by its sensitivity to market returns, then beta is a key determinant of value in pricing models for share or portfolio returns.

An investment's beta is expressed as a ratio of the market's beta, which is always 1.0. Therefore a share with a beta of 1.5 would be expected to rise 15% when the market goes up 10% and fall 15% when the market drops 10%. In technical terms, beta is calculated using a least-squared regression equation and it is the coefficient that defines the slope of the regression line on a chart measuring, say, the relative returns of a share and its underlying market. However, the beta values derived from the regression calculation can vary tremendously depending on the data used. A share's beta generated from weekly returns over, say, one year might be very different from the beta produced from monthly returns over five years.

This highlights a major weakness of beta: that it is not good at predicting future price volatility based on past performance. This is certainly true of individual shares. For portfolios of shares beta works better, basically because the effects of erratically changing betas on individual shares generally cancel each other out in a portfolio. Also, to the extent that portfolio theory is all about reducing risk through aggregating investments, beta remains a useful tool in price modelling.

Bid price

The price that a dealer will pay for securities in the market. Thus it is the lower of the two prices that the dealer will quote for any security. For a MUTUAL FUND, it is the price at which the fund management company will buy in units from investors. (See also OFFER PRICE and SPREAD.)

Big Bang

The event that took place on October 27th 1986 and transformed the way in which the LONDON STOCK EXCHANGE operated. It resulted from a deal between the government and the stock exchange in which the government dropped moves to challenge the exchange's restrictive practices in return for various liberalisation measures:

- The exchange scrapped the rules that its members had to be either wholesalers of shares (jobbers) or brokers who dealt directly with investors.
- Brokers became free to supply clients with shares held in their own account and they could, if they wished, become MARKETMAKERS in shares.
- Restrictions on ownership of exchange member firms were first relaxed and then dropped, unleashing a flood of money

into London as various financial conglomerates bought London jobbing and broking firms.

- A screen-based system of trading stocks (STOCK EXCHANGE AUTOMATED QUOTATIONS – SEAQ) closely modelled on the NASDAQ system was introduced, leading to the demise of floor trading on the exchange.

The abolition of exchange controls by the UK government in 1979 made these moves almost inevitable. The London market had to adapt to the globalisation of share trading or it would have become a backwater.

Big Board

Nickname for the NEW YORK STOCK EXCHANGE.

Binomial option pricing model

The basic principle behind this and other OPTION pricing models is that an option to buy or sell a specific STOCK can be replicated by holding a combination of the underlying stock and cash borrowed or lent. The idea is that the cash and security combined can be fairly accurately estimated and their combined value must equal the value of the option. This has to be so, otherwise there would be the opportunity to make RISK-free profits by switching between the two.

Take a simple example, the aim of which is to find the value today of a CALL OPTION on a COMMON STOCK that expires in one year's time. The current stock price is $100, as is the call's EXERCISE PRICE. To maintain clarity and avoid the complicating effect of an option's DELTA on the arithmetic involved, imagine that an investor holds just half of this stock (that is, $50-worth) in his portfolio. The portfolio's only other component is a SHORT position in a ZERO-COUPON BOND currently worth $42.45, which has to be repaid at $45 in a year's time.

Next assume that the value of the stock in a year's time will be either $110 or $90. From these two postulated outcomes several conclusions arise. First, we can value the call option in a year's time. It will be either $10 or zero. Second, we can value the portfolio. It too will be either $10 or zero. This must be so, since the value of the portfolio is the stock's value minus the debt on the zero-coupon bond. So it is either $55 minus $45, or $45 minus $45. The future value of the stock may be uncertain, but the value of the debt on the bond is not. Third, the alternative values for both the call option and the portfolio at the year end are the same. If this is so, then their start value must be the same as well. The start value for the portfolio can be easily calculated. It is $50 minus $42.45; that is, $7.55. So this must also be the present value of the call option.

From this basic building block of the binomial model comes the formula that the value of a call will be the current value of the stock in question multiplied by the option's delta (which, in effect, was 0.5 in our example) minus the borrowing needed to replicate the option. Using our example, the linear representation would be:

$$\text{Call value} = (\$100 \times 0.5) - \$42.45 = \$7.55$$

This is the single-period binomial model, so called because the starting point is to take two permitted outcomes for the stock price and then work back to find what this means for the present value of the option.

In the real world, however, a single-period model is not practical, hence the development of the multi-period binomial model where each period used to estimate the price of the option can be as short as computer power will allow. As the number of price outcomes rises by 2 to the power of the number of periods under review, the model is computer-intensive; a model using 20 periods, for example, would need over 1m calculations. Additionally, rather than using arbitrary stock-price outcomes from which to estimate the value of the option, the model takes advantage of the fact that, given an estimate of the rate at which a stock price will change, future stock prices can be estimated within a reasonable band of certainty using mathematical distribution tables.

The result is a model which produces options prices that closely mirror market prices. Furthermore, because the binomial model splits its calculations into tiny time portions, it can easily cope with the effect of dividends on stock prices and, hence, option values. This is an important factor with which the more widely used BLACK-SCHOLES OPTION PRICING MODEL copes less capably.

“*Men, it has been well said, think in herds; it will be seen that they go mad in herds while they only recover their senses slowly and one by one.*

Charles Mackay, *Extraordinary Popular Delusions and the Madness of Crowds*

Black Monday

Monday October 19th 1987 when Wall Street had its worst day since 1914. The DOW JONES INDUSTRIAL AVERAGE fell 508 points from 2,247 to 1,738, or 22.6%. This triggered panic selling in EQUITY markets around the world and, for example, on the same day the UK's FTSE ALL-SHARE INDEX fell 9.7% from 1,190 to 1,075, then dropped a further 11% the following day. Until that point 1987 had been a great year for equities. From the start of the year until its mid-August peak, the Dow rose 44%. However, rising interest rates caused investors to worry and the German Bundesbank's decision to increase its rates on October 16th was the cue for them to dash for the exit.

The Dow bounced back rapidly from its low. On October 26th

alone it put on 10%. The UK index, however, continued to fall and did not bottom out until December 3rd, when it closed at 750, 39% below its mid-year peak.

Black-Scholes option pricing model

A pricing model that ranks among the most influential. It was devised by Fischer Black and Myron Scholes, two Chicago academics, in 1973, the year that formalised options trading began on the CHICAGO BOARD OF TRADE. The Black-Scholes model, or adaptations of it, has gained universal acceptance for pricing options because its results are almost as good as those achieved by other options pricing models without the complexity.

Behind the model is the assumption that ASSET prices must adjust to prevent ARBITRAGE between various combinations of options and cash on the one hand and the actual asset on the other. Additionally, there are specific minimum and maximum values for an OPTION which are easily observable. Assuming, for example, that it is a CALL OPTION, then its maximum value must be the share price. Even if the EXERCISE PRICE is zero, no one will pay more than the share price simply to acquire the right to buy the shares. The minimum value, meanwhile, will be the difference between the share's price and the option's exercise price adjusted to its present value.

The model puts these fairly easy assumptions into a formula and then adjusts it to account for other relevant factors:

- The cost of money, because buying an option instead of the underlying STOCK saves money and, therefore, makes the option increasingly valuable the higher interest rates go.
- The time until the option expires, because the longer the period, the more valuable the option becomes since the option holder has more time in which to make a profit.

- The VOLATILITY of the underlying share price, because the more it is likely to bounce around, the greater chance the option holder has to make a profit.

Of these, volatility, as measured by the STANDARD DEVIATION of share returns, is the most significant factor. Yet it was the factor over which Black and Scholes struggled because it is not intuitively obvious that greater volatility should equal greater value. That it is so is because of the peculiar nature of options: they peg losses to the amount paid for the option, yet they offer unlimited potential for profit.

Note that the basic Black-Scholes model is for pricing a call option, but it can be readily adapted for pricing a PUT OPTION. It also ignores the effect on the price of the option of any dividends that are paid on the shares during the period until the option expires. This is remedied either by deducting the likely present value of any DIVIDEND from the share price that is input into the model, or by using a refinement of the Black-Scholes model which writes off the effect of the dividend evenly over the period until it is paid.

Bollinger bands

Used in TECHNICAL ANALYSIS to determine areas of support for and resistance to price changes. On a chart these plot the STANDARD DEVIATION of the moving average of a price. So when they are plotted above and below the moving average, the bands widen and narrow according to the underlying VOLATILITY of the average. The longer the period of low volatility, the closer together the lines become and the greater is the likelihood that there will be a break-out from the established price pattern.

Bond

Generic name for a tradable, long-term debt security raised by a borrower who agrees to make specific payments, usually regular payments of interest and repayment of principal on maturity. (See also TREASURY BOND, EUROBOND, GILT-EDGED STOCK.)

Bond rating

The chances that bonds of all types might go into default – that is, the borrower will fail to pay the interest and/or the capital due on a BOND – is rated by several credit organisations, the best known of which are Moody's, Standard & Poor's (S&P) and Fitch. Together these three dominate the market for providing credit ratings. Moody's and S&P use a similar system to rate the safety of a bond, primarily based on a detailed examination of the creditworthiness of the borrower and the terms of the bond. For S&P the credit rankings range from AAA (the best) to D, meaning that the bond is already in default. The Moody's ratings go from Aaa to D. However, only bonds with a rating of BBB or better (Baa in the case of Moody's) are considered "investment grade", that is, good enough for institutional investors. Bonds below these grades are colloquially termed junk bonds.

Both S&P's and Moody's bond ratings are monitored closely by investors and therefore any change in an issuer's ratings will be matched by a corresponding movement in the market price of its debt. However, during the CREDIT CRUNCH of 2008 agencies were fiercely criticised for failing to mark down the quality of debt obligations quickly enough and for being unduly influenced by the financial markets when making downgrades.

Bonus issue

A misleading euphemism for a CAPITALISATION ISSUE.

Book value

That part of a company's assets which belongs to its shareholders; in the UK these are generally known as shareholders' funds or, simply, net assets. Book value is an accounting valuation arrived at by taking the gross assets of a business as shown in its BALANCE SHEET and subtracting all the prior claims on the business, such as bank debt, payables, allowances for future claims, and so on. Alternatively, it is the sum of the shares outstanding, additional paid-in capital and retained EARNINGS. Book value is usually expressed in per share terms so as to make an easy comparison with the market price of the shares (see PRICE TO BOOK RATIO).

Bottom fishing

What value-seeking investors do after a stockmarket has fallen heavily, exposing good value in shares which fair-weather investors are still too shell-shocked to take.

Brady bond

Named after Nicholas Brady, an American Treasury secretary, who in 1989 came up with the Brady Plan to ease the debt burden that was crushing too many developing-country economies. Brady bonds are issued by indebted governments as part of a refinancing of their bank debt following the introduction of an agreed schedule between them and their creditors. This would be likely to include the adoption of responsible monetary policies by the governments concerned and some debt write-off by their bank lenders. Even so, Brady bonds, which are traded on OVER-THE-COUNTER markets, are high-RISK investments.

Buffett, Warren

The best-known investor on the planet whose net worth was estimated at around $60 billion at the end of 2007 by several sources. Buffett is known for the world-class returns he has produced for over 40 years from his investment conglomerate, Berkshire Hathaway, and for his insightful chairman's letter in Berkshire's ANNUAL REPORT. Adding in the investment record of Buffett's partnership, which he ran from 1956 to 1968 before sinking his capital into Berkshire, his record from 1956 to 2007 showed an annual compound growth rate of 22%, enough to turn $1,000 into $25m. Over the same period, the pre-tax return from the S&P 500 INDEX was 9.4% a year.

Buffett is characterised as an exponent of VALUE INVESTING and he learned his trade from Benjamin GRAHAM, who first espoused that particular cause. In many respects, however, Buffett's investment style is far removed from Graham's. It focuses on the "business franchise", the idea that there is a small cadre of exceptional businesses whose advantages mean that they are protected from everyday economics. Brand-name corporations, or those which can grow on the back of bigger corporations – "gross royalty businesses" such as advertising agencies – are good examples.

> *In the search for companies to acquire we adopt the same attitude one might find appropriate in looking for a spouse: it pays to be active, interested and open minded, but it does not pay to be in a hurry.*
>
> Warren Buffett, chairman, Berkshire Hathaway

Bull

An optimist; someone who assumes that prices will rise. The origin is unknown, although it probably evolved because it contrasts strongly with BEAR. As the quote from Alexander Pope shows, it was in common usage in London by the early 18th century.

“ *Come fill the South Sea goblet full;*
The Gods shall of our stock take care:
Europa pleased accepts the bull,
And Jove with joy puts off the bear.

Alexander Pope, inscription on a punch bowl, 1720
(the year of the South Sea Bubble)

Bulletin board

A website where investors post gossip, fact and opinion about stocks and markets. Bulletin boards are immensely popular, but – given their virtual anonymity and their lack of regulation – they can be traps for unwary investors.

CAC 40 Index

The most widely quoted measure of share prices on the PARIS BOURSE. The CAC 40 (CAC stands for either Compagnie Nationale des Agents de Change or Cotation Assistée en Continu – no one is sure now) was specifically developed as an index on which derivatives products could be based. It was introduced in 1988 with a base value of 1,000 for December 31st 1987 and comprises 40 of the 100 major stocks listed on the Paris market. During trading hours it is recalculated every time the price of one of its components changes.

Calendar effect

Ostensibly there is little logic to the idea that some times of the year, or even days of the week, should be better times to trade shares than others. Even so, many studies have noted clear patterns of calendar bias in share returns. The best known ones are as follows:

- **JANUARY EFFECT.** (See entry.)
- **Weekend effect.** Share prices tend to rise on Friday and fall on Monday.
- **Public holidays.** As in the weekend effect, shares tend to be stronger than average immediately before a public holiday (although not in the UK, according to one study).
- **Seasonal effects.** In the UK the months December–April tend to produce above-average returns and May–November below average, giving some credibility to the stockmarket saw: "Sell in May and go away."

> *October. This is one of the peculiarly dangerous months to speculate in stocks in. The others are July, January, September, April, November, May, March, June, December, August and February.*
>
> Mark Twain, *Pudd'nhead Wilson*

Call hedge

A strategy in options trading which protects a share or a portfolio against possible falls in market value. If an investor who holds a share, the price of which has risen substantially, fears for the share's short-term outlook, he may HEDGE (that is, insure) his position by writing a CALL OPTION against the share. Thus the investor would receive an underwriting fee. If the share's price subsequently falls, this would cover some or all of the losses sustained, depending on how thoroughly he had hedged his position. If, however, the share continues to rise, the investor would have to cancel his obligation to deliver shares by buying a matching call. He would make a loss on that transaction, but would still participate in the rise of the underlying STOCK.

Call option

A call is the right to buy an ASSET, probably an ORDINARY SHARE, for a specific price usually within a specified period, although just on a specific date if it is a "European-style" option.

To give a simple example, ignoring dealing costs, say an investor is bullish about the prospects for a particular share and buys a call option contract for 20p giving him the right to buy the share at 380p. Assume also that the market price of the share is 350p. If and when the share price rises above 400p the investor is in profit, having covered his 20p option price and the 380p EXERCISE PRICE. Although the price of the option will not move penny for penny with the price of the share, it will add considerable

LEVERAGE to his speculation. If the share trades at 450p when the contract expires, the investor would have made 50p for an outlay of 20p, a 150% profit. If, instead, the investor had bought the share for 350p, his profit would have been 100p, or 29%. Alternatively, the investor would lose money if the share price is less than 400p when the contract expires, and he would lose 100% of his cost if it is less than 380p. His maximum losses, however, are always pegged at 20p. Whereas if he bought the share at 350p and it fell to 300p his losses would be 50p, although only 14% in percentage terms.

Capital asset pricing model

Because of its comparative simplicity, the capital asset pricing model (CAP-M) is an influential formula for modelling the theoretically correct price of assets and portfolios. It developed out of PORTFOLIO THEORY in the 1960s, and, although the substantial body of academic research into its effectiveness increasingly draws critical conclusions, it remains an elegant theory which poses important questions about the extent to which investors can generate above-average returns from most investment selection techniques.

Basically, the CAP-M says that the return from an investment will equal the RISK-FREE RATE OF RETURN plus the excess return over the risk-free rate offered by the particular market in which the investment trades, in turn geared up by the sensitivity of the investment to market returns. For example, assume that the risk-free rate of return is 8% per year, that the market's return is 12% and that we are pricing a share whose sensitivity to the market is 1.2 times (that is, its historical returns have been 1.2 times whatever the market has done). The CAP-M would say that the share should return 12.8% (the calculation is $8 + 1.2 [12 - 8]$).

If this exercise were repeated for a variety of shares or portfolios of differing VOLATILITY in relation to the market, a line on a chart could be drawn showing the trade-off between return and volatility, which is known as the SECURITY MARKET LINE. If the line shows expected future returns it would slope upwards, indicating that as RISK (substituted here by volatility) increased, so investors would expect higher returns for their outlay.

This can be useful for testing whether some investments are cheap or expensive. Say that a share's expected risk/reward trade-off put it at a point above the security market line. It would be offering excess returns for a given level of risk and would, theoretically, be bought till the returns it offered future buyers were driven down to the market line. For a share which lay below the line the reverse would be true, and it would be sold till its expected returns rose to the market line.

Note that there are just three components in the formula and two of these – the risk-free return and the market's return – are the same for a given period whatever investments are being priced. The only variable factor in the equation, and thus a crucial one, is the sensitivity of the particular investment's returns to those of the market. This is measured by the investment's BETA. Suffice it to say here that beta is a flawed measure, which may give decent indications of the sensitivity for a portfolio of many investments, but which says little about the likely price volatility of a single security.

This only partially undermines the credibility of the CAP-M as a way of modelling prices. Exhaustive testing of the CAP-M using historical price data shows that investors were rewarded for holding securities which have above-average sensitivity to the market, even if they were not as well rewarded as the theory suggests they should have been. Furthermore, the failings of the CAP-M are not sufficiently great to confound the theory that investors are almost solely rewarded for assuming the risk that they cannot diversify away (that is, market or SYSTEMATIC RISK) and that, therefore, taking on diversifiable risk (UNSYSTEMATIC RISK) brings no obvious benefits.

> *The determination of the value of an item must not be based on its price, but rather on the utility that it yields. The price for the item is dependent only on the thing itself and is equal for everyone; the utility, however, is dependent on the particular circumstances of the person making the estimate.*
>
> Daniel Bernoulli, address to the Imperial Academy of Sciences, St Petersburg (1738)

Capital fulcrum point

An important formula for valuing a WARRANT, which measures the minimum annual percentage increase required from the value of the underlying ordinary shares for investors to hold warrants in a company's shares in preference to the shares themselves. If, for example, the capital fulcrum point were 8% but investors expected the shares in question to rise by 10% a year until the warrant's expiry date, they would choose the warrants because these would outperform the shares. If, however, investors expected the shares to rise by only 7%, these would be a better bet than the warrants. As such, the formula calculates the fulcrum point above which warrants, thanks to their LEVERAGE, become more attractive and below which ordinary shares are favoured.

The mathematical formula (see Appendix 5) works out the compound rate at which both the share price and the warrant price must grow in order for it to be equally advantageous for investors to hold either the shares or the warrants. Imagine the EXERCISE PRICE of the warrants is 100, the current share price is 145, the warrant price is 80 and the warrants expire in five years' time. By trial and error investors would eventually work out that the share price must grow by 9% a year to make it worthwhile holding the warrants to expiry. Any less than that would mean there was not enough INTRINSIC VALUE in the equation for the share price to pull the warrant price up at the same pace.

Share-price growth above 9% a year would mean that the intrinsic value would swell, thus the value of the warrants – because their price is lower than the share price – would have to rise faster than the shares in order to keep the equation in balance.

Besides helping comparisons between warrants and their underlying shares, the capital fulcrum point also allows comparisons between warrants with different expiry dates because it is expressed as a DISCOUNT RATE. Take warrants in two companies which have similar prospects. If one's fulcrum point was 7% and the other's was 9%, it would not matter how long each had to expiry; the likelihood is that the warrant with the 7% fulcrum point would be more attractive.

Capital gains tax

All the world's developed economies have a capital gains tax with which the profit on the sale of an ASSET is taxed. Among the tax's common characteristics are a facility to offset losses against gains for disposals made within the same tax period; an annual allowance, which means that gains up to a specified threshold are tax free (for example, as of 2008–09, the first £9,600 of gains in the UK); and tax rates that vary, depending on how long the disposed investment has been owned. For example, in the United States, gains on assets held for more than a year are taxed at 20% for a marginal-rate tax payer, but gains on assets held for less than a year are taxed at 27% or more. In the UK, from the income tax year 2008–09 the so-called "taper relief" was scrapped. In its place the government imposed a flat-rate tax of 18% on all profits realised on taxable assets regardless of how long they had been held.

Capital market line

The graphical depiction of the trade-off between RISK and return for an EFFICIENT PORTFOLIO. In other words, it is a chart line which shows how much extra return investors would expect for taking on extra risk. Prospectively, the chart line must slope upwards (investors would not assume extra risk if they thought they were not going to get extra reward), although actual returns show that it can slope downwards for a while. This means that in the real world investors are not always rewarded for taking on higher risks. Logically this must be so; otherwise so-called higher risks would not really exist.

Arithmetically, it is calculated by taking the EQUITY RISK PREMIUM on a portfolio and dividing this by the amount of risk within the portfolio in question. So if the EXPECTED RETURN on the market were 8% and the RISK-FREE RATE OF RETURN were 5%, the risk premium would be 3%. Then, if the portfolio's risk, as calculated by its STANDARD DEVIATION, were 15%, the capital market line would be $(8 - 5) \div 15$, which equals 0.2%. This means that for every 1% increase in a portfolio's risk, the market would demand a 0.2% risk premium.

Capital market theory

The generic term for those models that aim to price assets, usually marketable securities or portfolios of them, in terms of the trade-off between RISK and return that PORTFOLIO THEORY assumes all investors seek. The best known, and most influential, of these is the CAPITAL ASSET PRICING MODEL.

Capitalisation issue

See SCRIP ISSUE.

Capitalise

Something that companies do to costs to the benefit of immediate profits but often to the detriment of the state of the BALANCE SHEET. To capitalise is to treat a cost incurred as part of the future capital value of an ASSET. Therefore, instead of charging it against the INCOME STATEMENT, it is added to both sides of the balance sheet and written off against profits in future accounting periods.

CAP-M

See CAPITAL ASSET PRICING MODEL.

Carried interest

The fee that the managers of partnerships receive for performance above a specified threshold. Carried interest has attracted controversy in both the United States and the UK in the context of the huge rewards made by the managers of PRIVATE EQUITY funds and, to a lesser extent, HEDGE FUNDS. The root of the problem is that carried interest looks very much like income yet, thanks to anomalies in the personal tax regimes of both the United States and the UK, it is taxed as a capital gain at lower rates than income. The especially low rates of tax on some forms of capital gains in the UK prompted one private equity manager to comment – candidly – that he paid less tax than his cleaner. As a result, reforms have been made to the UK's CAPITAL GAINS TAX regime and similar proposals have been aired in the United States.

Cash flow

Ultimately companies are processors of cash. Cash comes in and cash goes out and companies must bring in more than they expend in order to survive. The cash flow statement, also called the funds flow statement, in a company's accounts shows how a company achieves this from year to year. In so doing, the cash statement does two other things: roughly speaking, it reconciles the income shown in the INCOME STATEMENT with the movement of cash within the business; and, equally approximately, it reconciles the BALANCE SHEET from the start to the end of the financial year in question.

Common sense says that cash flow must be about the cash that a company brings in, from selling its goods and services and by other means, and the cash that it pays out, to suppliers, to other creditors and to providers of capital. The way that cash flow is generally shown in UK and US company accounts, however, is more about reconciling the profits or losses shown in the income statement with changes in the business's underlying cash position. To do this, the cash flow statement takes net income and adds back some major non-cash items that have been charged against the income account; namely, DEPRECIATION and increases in deferred taxes. In the United States, in particular, the vagueness of the relevant accounting standard means that it is often not clear how much of a company's cash flow really is in cash.

For the investor, though, the challenge is to use the cash flow statement to get a feel for how a company is funding its dividends (since they must be paid in cash) and whether it is generating enough cash internally to fund its future growth.

CDO

See COLLATERALISED DEBT OBLIGATION.

CFD

See CONTRACT FOR DIFFERENCE.

Chartist

Someone who uses TECHNICAL ANALYSIS to forecast the future price changes of a marketable investment.

> *A chartist must, like the oracle of Delphi, be constantly on call with predictive aphorisms, which does produce cult and cant.*
>
> "Adam Smith", *The Money Game*

Chicago Board of Trade

A financial exchange which claims to be the world's oldest FUTURES and OPTIONS and exchange. In July 2007 the Chicago Board of Trade (CBOT) was taken over by the CHICAGO MERCANTILE EXCHANGE in an $8 billion all-share transaction to become part of the enlarged CME Group. Until then, the CBOT had been owned by its members for the first 157 years of its history and had a short period – 2005–07 – when its shares were listed on the NEW YORK STOCK EXCHANGE.

It was founded in 1848 and introduced futures contracts in grain in 1864. In 1898 it spun off the Chicago Butter and Egg Board, which changed its name to the Chicago Mercantile Exchange in 1919 when it, too, introduced futures trading.

The CBOT continues to use a trading floor where OPEN OUTCRY trading takes place, but increasingly trading is via an electronic system. About three-quarters of trading is in interest rate products, and trading in commodities accounts for about one-fifth.

Chicago Mercantile Exchange

The "Merc" is the world's biggest FUTURES exchange in term of OPEN INTEREST (the number of futures contracts outstanding at the end of any trading day). Its biggest day in 2006 was September

14th when 105m positions were open at the end of the day. In contrast, the biggest day in 2000, a comparatively quiet year, produced just 9.3m open positions. Its trading focuses on four main product areas: interest rates, stockmarket indices, foreign exchange and commodities (its original product). It also offers more exotic futures, namely real estate and the weather (including frost and snowfall in the United States).

The Merc was founded in 1874 and spun off from the CHICAGO BOARD OF TRADE (CBOT) in 1898. However, it merged with the CBOT once more in 2007 when the two organisations formed CME Group, to which was added the New York Mercantile Exchange in 2008. A driving factor behind these deals was to provide trading volumes for CME Globex, the Merc's electronic trading system, which was introduced in 1992 and has increasingly taken the place of OPEN OUTCRY trading.

Chinese wall

Walls that certainly do not exist structurally and, some might suggest, not even figuratively, as they are supposed to. A Chinese wall is there to stop confidential, price-sensitive information flowing from one part of a financial institution to others where its knowledge might at best compromise or, at worst, give unfair profit opportunities to a privileged few. Most importantly, Chinese walls surround the corporate finance department of an investment bank where corporate deals are planned long before they are announced. Such information, for example, needs to be kept from the bank's fund management arm, where managers would be tempted to profit from it, and from its stockbroking operation, where sales staff might tell their own clients about it.

Chinese walls are maintained by a combination of the threat of penalties for those who are found breaking the rules and the integrity of the staff involved. Given that it is so difficult to find the source when confidential information has actually leaked out, the wonder is that Chinese walls are not breached more often.

Circuit breaker

A stock exchange regulation to limit or postpone share trading in response to a sharp movement in the cash market or its corresponding FUTURES market. On the NEW YORK STOCK EXCHANGE circuit breakers are fine-tuned every quarter with the aim of halting trading on the following basis:

- If the DOW JONES INDUSTRIAL AVERAGE falls 10% within a trading day, trading is stopped for one hour.
- If the Dow falls 20% in a trading day, trading is stopped for two hours.
- If the Dow falls 30% in a day, trading is stopped for the remainder of the day.

The rules may seem somewhat academic given that the circuit breaker has only been triggered once since it was introduced in 1987. That was October 27th 1997, when the trigger levels were lower and the Dow fell 7% on the day. In fact, the Dow has dropped 10% or more in a day just three times in its history.

The specific number of points fall in the Dow needed to trigger a circuit break is set in January, April, July and October, based on the closing values of the index for the previous month. (See also TRADING COLLAR.)

Closed-end fund

Known as an investment trust in the UK, a closed-end fund, like its MUTUAL FUND cousin, offers private investors the means to acquire a diversified portfolio of investments for a much smaller outlay than if they were investing directly. However, the structure of closed-end funds means they offer more than this. The "closed-end" in the title refers to the fact that closed-end funds are companies with ordinary shares that trade on a stockmarket like any other listed company. Thus the number of "units" into which a closed-end fund's portfolio is divided is fixed, unless the fund has a new share issue. For investors, therefore, putting money into a closed-end fund, or taking it out, means dealing in existing shares on a stock exchange.

Closed-end funds can, however, gain access to new capital by borrowing. In so doing, they can LEVERAGE returns for their shareholders. To do this successfully they must achieve overall investment returns greater than their cost of borrowing, otherwise the leverage works against the shareholders.

Leverage comes in a more exotic form, too: the dual-purpose fund (or split capital investment trust in the UK). In this case the fund's capital is structured to give some classes of shareholders priority over others in their claims on the portfolio's income and/or assets. Because dual-purpose funds must have a fixed life until liquidation (how else could claims on their assets be realised?) there is another effect. There is a reduction in the discount to their pro-rata portfolio value at which most closed-end fund shares trade on the stockmarket. This will not always be the case for all classes of shares in a dual-purpose fund, but it will be true for the market value of the fund's shares compared with the market value of the underlying portfolio.

Why so many funds trade at less than their net asset value remains a mystery. Various theories are advanced:

- that the effect of fund management charges (and sometimes the ability of fund managers) is to subtract value from the portfolio;
- that closed-end funds do not distribute all the income their portfolios generate, therefore a DIVIDEND DISCOUNT MODEL will value them at less than that of the underlying portfolio;

- that there are simply too many such funds, so laws of supply and demand dictate that for many a discount is the only price at which trades can clear. The fact that some specialist funds trade at a premium to their portfolio value gives some credence to this possibility.

Coin-flipping contest

An analogy that helps to justify the EFFICIENT MARKET HYPOTHESIS. Imagine that 220m citizens of the United States are all arranged into a knock-out coin-flipping contest. Each contestant who calls correctly moves to the next round; the losers are eliminated. After 25 rounds there would be just six contestants left – contestants who had done nothing exceptional except guess correctly on which side a coin was going to land. However, they might seem special because, of the 220m who started, they are the only ones who called correctly 25 times running.

By the same token, those fund managers who produce outstanding investment returns year-in, year-out may be doing nothing more than correctly guessing which shares to buy and sell. On this logic the existence of just a few investors with a record of consistent excellence does not undermine the efficient market hypothesis but is actually consistent with it, since their numbers are so few as to be in line with the numbers that chance would produce.

Collateralised debt obligation

The security that has been at the heart of the credit crisis that rocked the world's financial markets from summer 2007 onwards. Like so many financial innovations, only the packaging of collateralised debt obligations (CDOs) was new and, in effect, they relied on the old trick of using LEVERAGE to pay attractive returns.

Essentially a CDO is a portfolio of fixed-interest assets (usually mortgages and bank loans) whose interest income and risk of default are packaged into different tranches and sold to investors. Thus the lowest risk – and consequently the lowest YIELD – is parcelled into the senior tranche, which typically gets an AAA credit rating (see BOND RATING); and the highest risk – and therefore the highest yield – is attached to the junior or equity tranche, which is also known as "toxic waste".

However, the big attraction for investors is that by pooling asset-backed loans and mortgages CDOs can offer them higher yields than those available on conventional bonds of a similar risk. During a period of low or falling interest rates this feature was attractive indeed and issuance of CDOs mushroomed from $157 billion in 2004 to $489 billion in 2006, according to the Securities Industry and Financial Markets Association.

However, the complexity of CDOs – especially the more exotic variety, such as CDO-squared or CDO-cubed – meant that their risks were difficult to quantify. Thus when interest rates started to rise in 2007 and defaults grew in the underlying loans in CDO portfolios, the book losses that the owners of CDOs – mostly banks – had to declare were enormous. This played a big part in the paralysis of the world's credit markets.

Common stock

US terminology for ORDINARY SHARE.

Compound return

The return from an investment that includes the effect of DIVIDENDS or interest added to the original sum. Thus the compound rate of interest on a savings account assumes that periodically interest earned is added to the original principal and future interest is earned on both principal and interest earned. In most investment calculations, compounding periods are a year (that is, the rate is expressed per year), but compounding periods can be for any length of time. The compound rate of return is the GEOMETRIC MEAN.

> *Compound interest – the greatest invention of all time*
> Albert Einstein

Contract for difference

An enormously popular and useful innovation that began in London in the early 1990s and has spread to many different types of assets and to many financial centres.

A contract for difference (CFD) is an agreement between two parties that the seller of the CFD will pay the buyer the difference between the price of an ASSET at the start of the contract and its price when settlement is made. Beyond that, however, the CFD may become more complicated because it is possible to take both long and short positions in the underlying asset in question (though not both in the same contract) and the contract will have no specified expiry date. The absence of an expiry date means that the holder of a CFD to buy an asset will pay the seller a daily financing charge, which tracks the market value of the asset, and the holder of a CFD to sell an asset may receive an interest payment in lieu of the interest that could be generated from the sale proceeds. Moreover, to the extent that CFDs in an individual company's shares seek to replicate ownership of the share, holders of a contract to buy shares will receive such DIVIDENDS as are paid in respect of the shares while the contract is outstanding. Likewise, holders of a CFD to sell shares will pay the dividends. Lastly, because transactions in CFDs contain lots of LEVERAGE, contracts require the buyer to post MARGIN. There is both an initial payment of between 5% and 30% of the contract's value and a MARK TO MARKET payment that takes account of daily price changes in the contract's underlying value.

CFDS are now available globally, though not in the United States where they fall foul of the SECURITIES AND EXCHANGE COMMISSION rules on DERIVATIVES. They are available not just for individual shares but also for major stockmarket indices, commodities, government bonds and currencies.

Convertible

A derivative before the term DERIVATIVES was invented. Convertibles are hybrid securities – part BOND, part ORDINARY SHARE – which are issued by companies to raise capital. They come in two forms: convertible shares (convertible bonds in the United States) and convertible preference shares (convertible PREFERRED STOCK in the United States). They breeze in and out of fashion, being favoured by the companies that issue them when interest rates are high because the OPTION to convert into ordinary shares means that they carry lower interest rates than straight debt. Investors favour them when stockmarket values look shaky because they are protected by the debt characteristics in convertibles while simultaneously retaining an exposure to shares should the market recover.

Because convertibles are essentially low-coupon bonds with embedded CALL OPTIONS, they can be valued using option valuation techniques. This is fraught with difficulties, however, particularly because the effective EXERCISE PRICE of the option changes with the market price of the convertible. In practice, therefore, convertibles are usually valued as EQUITY with an income advantage. Take a simplified example of a company which has convertible shares outstanding with a 6.5% COUPON and a final conversion date sufficiently far off not to be material. Assume also that the convertibles trade in the market at $80 for every $100 nominal of

STOCK – which means that their DIVIDEND YIELD is 8.2% – and that their conversion terms are ten shares for every $100 nominal. Meanwhile, the share has a market price of $5 and its yield is 4%.

The price of the convertibles therefore comprises two components: the underlying value of the shares into which they can convert and the income advantage they offer over holding the shares. In this example, the underlying conversion value is $50; this is fairly obvious since one bond has the right to convert into ten ordinary shares which are currently valued at $5 each. The remaining $30 is the market's estimate of the extra income in today's money values that comes from holding a bond whose coupon is fixed compared with shares whose DIVIDENDS should grow.

Whether that $30 is a good estimate depends on how fast dividends on the shares are expected to grow. If they manage just over 10% a year, it is a good estimate, because it will be almost eight years before the shares offer an income advantage, by which time holders of the convertibles will have accumulated about $30 of extra income at today's values.

If dividends on the shares grow faster than that, however, less excess income will accumulate to holders of the convertibles before it is time to convert. If they grow at 15% a year, for example, only about $25 extra would accrue. In this case, the convertible would be worth only $75 ($50 of convertible value plus the income differential). Investors who expected such pacey growth in share dividends would, therefore, sell the convertible and buy the shares until the gap had been closed.

Corporate filing

All well-developed securities industries demand that every company whose securities are traded on a recognised stock exchange must formally disclose relevant information about such things as the nature and performance of the business; financial accounts; the capital structure of the company and any changes to it; material changes to the assets of the company; offers to sell new securities in the company; offers to purchase the existing securities of the company.

In the United States such information is filed with the SECURITIES AND EXCHANGE COMMISSION, which demands a whole raft of reports. The most important ones are as follows:

- 10-K – filed annually; a comprehensive overview of the company.
- 10-Q – the quarterly financial report filed by the company.
- 8K – a report of unscheduled material events (in particular, acquisition or disposal of assets).
- 14D-1 – filed by a company making a tender offer for shares in a target company.
- 14D-9 – filed by the management of a company in receipt of a tender offer from another.
- 20-F – the ANNUAL REPORT filed by foreign companies whose securities are listed on a US exchange.

Corporate governance

The way in which companies run themselves; in particular, the way in which they are accountable to those who have a vested interest in their performance, especially their shareholders. Since the mid-1980s the issue has been controversial, made so by the wave of takeover activity in both the UK and the United States from that time on and by the trend for senior executives effectively to pay themselves huge amounts that too often have little correlation with the performance of the business.

This situation arose because of laws that limited the power of shareholders in the United States and liquid stockmarkets that made it easier for shareholders to sell shares in problem companies rather than stay and resolve difficulties. However, the reaction is now well established, with various shareholder pressure groups in both the UK and the United States urging restructured boards on to companies and demanding that senior executives' pay be more closely and formally linked to corporate performance. In the UK four committees – the Cadbury Committee, Greenbury Committee, Hampel Committee and Higgs Committee – have made recommendations that effectively have the force of law behind them.

> *Is not commercial credit based primarily upon money or property?" "No sir, the first thing is character."*
>
> J. Pierpont Morgan, to the House Banking and Currency Committee, 1913

Corporate social responsibility

How companies behave responsibly – not just to the extent that they act within the law, which is a given, but the way in which they manage their relations with so-called stakeholders, other than their shareholders. Such stakeholders include employees but, more importantly perhaps, people and the environment in general.

The growth of corporate social responsibility (CSR) has paralleled the growth of environmental issues, but there is more to CSR for companies than simply monitoring – and reducing – their CO_2 emissions.

Broadly, CSR comes under four headings:

- being a good corporate citizen, especially with regard to the environment;
- engaging in corporate philanthropy, which increasingly goes beyond simply donating money to good causes and entails getting actively involved (seconding employees to non-profit organisations, for example);
- protecting the company's reputation by being seen to work responsibly;

- somehow adding value to the company by doing good (the most contentious issue).

It remains debatable whether CSR is anything more than glorified public relations. That said, the debate about whether companies should get involved in CSR is pretty well over. Nowadays, involvement in CSR is also a given.

Counterparty

The party on the other side of a transaction. In the world's financial markets this means it is the party that agrees to deliver or to take delivery of a specific ASSET at a particular date and price. Counterparty RISK is a spectre that haunts the global financial system – the fear that a counterparty will fail to honour its obligations and in so doing trigger a systemic collapse where one failure leads to many. One of the big advantages of trading on a recognised stock exchange is that the exchange itself usually occupies the position of counterparty to each transaction, thus minimising this risk. OVER-THE-COUNTER markets, however, have no such fail-safe mechanism.

Coupon

The fixed periodic interest payable on a BOND, so-called because originally, and sometimes still, the security certificate had a series of counterfoils – or coupons – which were detached in return for the interest payment.

Covariance

A crucial part of PORTFOLIO THEORY because it helps quantify the RISK in a portfolio – that is, the likelihood that the portfolio's returns will be less than expected. Risk is therefore determined by how volatile the returns of each of the portfolio's components are, or are likely to be. In addition, and more importantly, it is necessary to have a factor which measures the relative movements of each pair of investments within the portfolio because risk is reduced by the extent to which returns on any component in the portfolio move in opposite directions to the other components. This is the function of covariance.

The covariances of investments therefore can be as follows:

- Positive, meaning that the investments move in the same direction as each other.
- Negative, meaning that they move in opposite directions; that is, when the returns from one rise, returns from the other fall.
- Zero, meaning that the investments have no observable relation to each other.

In a theoretical world, a portfolio of investments with perfect negative covariance would eliminate risk. In the real world, however, investments – certainly securities – to an extent move in the same direction. That is, there is some positive covariance. This means that risk can be reduced but not completely eliminated.

Covered option

An OPTION is covered if an investor who underwrites a call owns the STOCK in question. This means that if the stock is "called away" from him, the investor is covered against any losses necessitated by having to buy the stock in the market. Thus the WRITER is betting against the price of the underlying security rising much during the option's term. If that bet proves right, the writer's own investment return will be enhanced by the receipt of the fee for writing the call.

Covered warrant

A cross between a WARRANT and a TRADED OPTION. Demand for covered warrants came from institutional investors which wanted more DERIVATIVES products than were available on recognised stock exchanges. Thus an OVER-THE-COUNTER market grew up in which institutions issued and traded covered warrants, giving the buyer the right but not the obligation to buy an ASSET (usually a company security) at a pre-set price within a specified period (usually up to three years – longer than the term offered by traded options but shorter than the term for conventional warrants issued by companies in their own name).

The term "covered" denoted that the issuing institution held the shares in which it issued warrants and was therefore covered against any call. However, this soon became a misnomer as warrant issues were often only partially covered, or not covered at all. It also became a misnomer in the sense that covered warrants were available as puts, which gave the holder the right to sell the underlying security.

As a result of the growing popularity of covered warrants, it is now more sensible to see them as long-dated options, which are increasingly exchange traded, regulated by the appropriate national investment authority and almost always settled for cash rather than the underlying security.

Credit crunch

Generically, a credit crunch is much the same as a credit squeeze, where the availability of short-term loans of various sorts becomes restricted. As a result, there are business failures and possibly the failure of banks too as their inability to renew their own lines of credit prompts a run on their retail deposits. More specifically, if the crisis in the world's financial markets that began in the summer of 2007 goes by any shorthand name, it is the credit crunch.

While the effects of this particular crisis have spread far beyond the banking industry, they were first felt as a fairly conventional tightening of credit availability in the wholesale money markets where banks lend to each other. This coincided with a rise in interest rates in the United States which filtered through to the cost of house-purchase mortgages. As a result, the rate at which borrowers were defaulting on the interest payments on their mortgages began to rise to worrying levels. This quickly eroded confidence in bundles of such mortgages that were used both as collateral for interbank loans and as the raw material for securitised products of many varieties. This reluctance to accept tranches of mortgages as security for loans led directly to the first major casualty of the credit crunch. In September 2007, Northern Rock, a British mortgage bank that relied on the wholesale money markets for its funds, had to be rescued – and later nationalised – by the UK government.

The effects of the credit crunch widened and deepened in 2008 as, in March, Bear Stearns, a US investment bank, had to be rescued; this was followed in September by the nationalisation of Fannie Mae and Freddie Mac, major US institutions that bought or guaranteed existing mortgages. Almost simultaneously, the US authorities bailed out America's biggest insurance group, AIG, which was running up huge losses from underwriting – that is, insuring – credit-default SWAPS, which protected other parties, mostly banks, against defaults in their loan portfolios. Also in that month the authorities allowed the failure of the fourth biggest investment bank, Lehman Brothers, on the implicit grounds that to rescue it would encourage moral hazard elsewhere in the banking system. Quickly that looked a bad decision because of Lehman's prominent position in the so-called shadow banking system where the broking arms of investment banks supplied liquidity to all manner of investment funds. With unquantifiable billions of dollars-worth of assets locked up in Lehman's broking operation, its demise further clogged up the money markets.

Within the space of a few weeks in September and October 2008 the credit crunch morphed into the biggest economic crisis to confront the developed world since the depression of the 1930s. The response of Treasury departments and central banks in the United States and Europe was on a scale not seen before. By early 2009, the central bank lending rate in the United States – the Fed Funds Rate – was effectively zero and the Bank of England's base rate was 0.5%, as low as it had ever been in the bank's 300-year history.

Whether the authorities' response – loosening both fiscal and monetary policy – was the right one remains to be seen. However, as the enormity of the credit crunch expanded, so did the number of factors that were gathered together to explain it. Conventional wisdom now says the roots of the crisis lay in the huge trade imbalances between the developed world, especially the United States, which ran deficits, and the developing world, especially China and the oil-exporting countries, which ran surpluses. The cash from those surpluses had to go somewhere and – for safety's sake – it tended to be recycled back to the developed world, in particular the United States, where it helped to keep interest rates abnormally low and to fund vast and fast-rising borrowings by consumers.

This consumer binge was aided by governments and central banks, which both encouraged banks to provide mortgage finance to borrowers who in the past would have been considered too risky to lend to and kept short-term interest rates lower than they should have been. And it was abetted by the financial innovation of banks, which invented products that parcelled up lots of risky loans and, in so doing, theoretically lessened the effect of individual defaults. Into the mix then came ratings agencies, which were paid by banks to provide quality stickers for such products. It was not that the ratings agencies failed in their task, despite the obvious conflict of interests. Rather, the problem was that too much product of supposedly good quality was being issued and then held by investors who did not know its provenance in sufficient detail. Thus, when doubts started to spread about securitised products, there was no telling the good quality stuff from the dross. As a result, the whole market failed.

> *A sound banker, alas, is not one who foresees danger and avoids it but one who, when he is ruined, is ruined in a conventional way along with his fellows so no one can really blame him.*
>
> John Maynard Keynes

Credit derivative

A generic term for a range of DERIVATIVES that are essentially insurance policies. At its simplest, a credit derivative would be a contract between two parties where one party buys protection against a specific event, or events, taking place and the other party sells protection. So in a credit-default SWAP, which is the most widely used form of credit derivative, the buyer would receive protection against something happening to a so-called reference entity. If the reference entity were a corporate BOND and the issuer of the bond breached its terms - say the underlying company went bust - then the buyer of protection would receive a contingent payment from the seller.

From that basic model credit derivatives take many forms, such as total-return swaps, credit-linked notes and synthetic COLLATERISED DEBT OBLIGATIONS, which offer exposure to many bonds within a single debt instrument.

Crest

An electronic means of settling share transactions and registering investors on companies' lists of shareholders, introduced into the UK in 1996. The effect of Crest is that ownership of company STOCK is treated much like money in a bank account, with information held and transactions booked electronically. Thus share certificates, much loved by many investors but of limited use because they do not actually confer ownership of a company's shares, effectively become a thing of the past.

CSR

See CORPORATE SOCIAL RESPONSIBILITY.

Cum-dividend

Stockmarket jargon which says that anyone buying particular shares is entitled to receive the next DIVIDEND that the issuer declares on those shares. Thus the market's estimate of the value of the dividend is included in the share price. (See also EX-DIVIDEND.)

Cum-rights

A share trades in the market cum-rights when the right to buy new shares in a RIGHTS ISSUE is still attached to it. (See also EX-RIGHTS.)

Data mining

Trawling through investment statistics, of which there are masses, to find patterns that suggest a theory, then propounding the theory. Such an approach – although widely and understandably used, given the volume of investment data and the power of today's computers – is potentially flawed because it finds the facts first then seeks to build the theory round them. Logically, it is more convincing to come up with an idea as to why something might happen and then see if the data bear it out. Some of the stockmarket anomalies which indicate that excess returns can be made by following particular trading routines are largely the product of data mining (see CALENDAR EFFECT).

DAX 30

Formerly the Deutsche Aktienindex, this is the leading index of German shares, comprising 30 blue-chip shares traded on the FRANKFURT STOCK EXCHANGE. It has a base value of 1,000 as at December 31st 1987 and, during trading hours, its value is calculated every minute.

Day trading

An investment tactic that gained popularity – and then notoriety – during the tech-stock bubble of the late 1990s. Day trading involves buying and holding securities for a very short time, sometimes just minutes, in order to make a quick profit. The theory is that if this is done repeatedly and with discipline, excess returns can be made. The practice began with institutional investors, but the spread of internet technology extended it to private investors, many of whom naively believed that this was the smartest way to invest. It may have been smart for the specialist firms that sold or rented day traders their equipment, or for the brokers through whom the traders dealt. But there is no conclusive evidence that day traders on average made excess returns and, indeed, the BEAR market of 2000–02 caused a sharp fall in this activity.

Dead cat bounce

An expression much favoured by market traders in the wake of the October crash of 1987. The analogy is between the reactions of the stockmarket and what would happen to a cat if it were dropped from the 40th floor of a tower block. On hitting the ground the cat would bounce, but it would still be dead. With such black humour did traders proffer their opinion of market rallies during that period.

Dead cross

A decidedly bearish sign for a CHARTIST. It occurs when a shorter moving average for the price of a marketable investment (say, the 20-day rolling average) falls below a longer moving average (say, 50 days). The signal is much stronger if the dead cross happens after the moving averages have moved in tandem for a period, as it implies a marked change in investors' attitudes.

Debenture

A long-term, marketable, FIXED-INCOME SECURITY issued by a company and secured against the assets of the company. In the UK a debenture is usually secured against specific assets; in the United States it is usually a floating charge on the assets in general. In either case, in the event of default on interest payments, debenture holders could force the company into liquidation. If the company had issued more than one class of debenture, however, there would be a pecking order for claims on the assets.

Deeply discounted rights issue

The practice whereby a company raises new capital through a RIGHTS ISSUE but issues new shares at a price far below the market price of its existing shares. Typically, in a rights issue, new shares will be sold at a discount of around 20% to the market price. In a deeply discounted rights issue, the discount may be 50% or more. Issuing companies and their advisers usually portray this as a golden opportunity to buy bargain shares in the company. However, there is no such thing as a cheap rights issue (see definition on page 200); the real reason for using a deeply discounted issue is more cynical. Essentially, it twists shareholders' arms to take up the new shares. If they don't, and they sell their rights entitlement, this will count as a part disposal of shares and may crystallise a CAPITAL GAINS TAX liability. Thus assured of an acceptable take-up of new shares, the issuing company can dispense with the costs of underwriting the issue (that is, insuring it against failure).

Delta

For speculators, one attraction of an OPTION is that it offers lots of LEVERAGE. However, the price changes of options do not follow changes in the price of the shares over which they have rights penny for penny. The price relationship between shares and their options is measured by an option's delta. This indicates the amount that the price of an option will move for a given change in the price of its underlying STOCK. Say that past observations had measured the delta as 0.6. Then a 10p change in the price of the share could be expected to produce a 6p change in the price of the option.

For a CALL OPTION the delta will always be positive, but for a PUT OPTION it will be negative. This is logical, since the price of the put will move in the opposite direction to changes in the share's price. (See HEDGE RATIO.)

Depreciation

The idea behind depreciation (known as amortisation in the United States) within a company's INCOME STATEMENT is simple and sensible enough. Its application, however, probably gives more scope for fudged figures than any other accounting item. This in turn complicates the job of assessing the value of a company's shares.

The basic idea is that the cost of a piece of capital equipment to a company should be written off over its useful life, not during the year in which the cost is incurred. This is sensible. A company's capital spending may vary considerably from one year to the next, but the flows of revenue from the equipment bought should be smoother, so it is better to align the two as far as possible.

One problem arises from estimating how long the equipment will last. If the estimate is a rotten one, then implicitly the depreciation charge will be meaningless as well. Using broad-brush depreciation rates for various classes of assets solves this problem, but only partially. Then there is the effect of changes to rates of depreciation. Lengthen the economic life of an ASSET and, other things being equal, you cut the depreciation charged against the asset, thus boosting profits. Or the method of calculating depreciation may be changed from one year to the next. Most companies depreciate on a straight-line basis; that is, they write off the same sum each year. If an asset under review looks less valuable than previously thought, some form of accelerated depreciation (double declining balance, sum of years digits, and so on) must be used to bring the asset down to its economic value. The effect is to make an assessment of a company's true profitability more difficult. Similarly, different depreciation policies among companies in the same industry make investment comparisons trickier.

The task for an investor is to cut through these accounting obfuscations. Make sure that the depreciation provisions are conservative and apply uniform depreciation rates in comparative studies is the sound advice of Benjamin GRAHAM and David Dodd's SECURITY ANALYSIS.

Derivatives

The generic name for financial products which are derived from other financial products and, according to some, threaten to bring chronic instability to the world's financial system. All derivatives contracts – whether they are OPTIONS, FUTURES, SWAPS or products with more exotic names – give one party the right (or at least the option) to make a claim on an underlying ASSET at some point in the future and bind another party to meet a counter-balancing obligation. The underlying product might be an ORDINARY SHARE, a stockmarket index, a commodity, a string of interest payments – the list goes on.

From this, two things follow. First, derivatives can offer insurance for the buyers of contracts because they take the uncertainty out of the future value of an asset. Second, derivatives offer lots of RISK – that is, the potential to make large losses as well as large gains – for someone who does not have a cash position to HEDGE because, in return for a comparatively small payment upfront, that party accepts the consequences of what transpires in the future.

Derivatives are traded either on a recognised exchange, such as the CHICAGO MERCANTILE EXCHANGE and EURONEXT, or OVER-THE-COUNTER (OTC), mainly by banks. In the case of exchange trading, the exchange places itself between all market participants and therefore accepts the risks of a counterparty defaulting. In the case of OTC trading, the obligations lie with the specific parties to a contract, making OTC derivatives – implicitly at least – a greater threat to financial stability because of the panic that might ensue if, say, a major bank did default on its commitments.

> *There are two times in a man's life when he shouldn't speculate. When he can't afford it and when he can.*
>
> Mark Twain, *Following the Equator*

Deutsche Börse

The holding company that runs the FRANKFURT STOCK EXCHANGE, which is by far the largest of Germany's seven regional stock exchanges with a 90% share of turnover. Deutsche Börse also owns Xetra, an electronic platform for trading securities that was introduced in 1997, EUREX, a derivatives exchange which is a joint venture with the Swiss FUTURES exchange, and Clearstream, which provides settlement services for securities transactions and custodian services.

In the early 2000s, Deutsche Börse's rise seemed inexorable as it added key features, such as DERIVATIVES trading and settlement, to its range of services. Since then, however, it has twice tried and failed to merge with the LONDON STOCK EXCHANGE – in 2001 and 2006 – and in 2008 lost out to the NEW YORK STOCK EXCHANGE in its attempt to merge with EURONEXT, which would have created by far the biggest financial exchange on mainland Europe.

Deutsche Terminbörse

Germany's fast-growing DERIVATIVES exchange, which is run by the DEUTSCHE BÖRSE and which merged with the Swiss futures exchange, Soffex, to form EUREX in 1998.

Dilution

What happens when an EQUITY shareholder's interest in a business is reduced by the issue of new shares to outside investors. A shareholder's PRE-EMPTION RIGHTS mean that excessive dilution can normally only take place with the permission of existing shareholders. However, small-scale dilution continually occurs – for example, through converting executives' OPTIONS into new shares or issuing new shares up to an annual limit that shareholders have authorised in advance.

Dilution also refers to a reduction in shareholders' pro-rata entitlement to a company's profits caused by the acquisition of a new business. In this context, company bosses almost always reassure existing shareholders that the transaction will not dilute growth in EARNINGS per share – that is, earnings per share will not be less than they would have been had the acquisition not taken place. This may be scant reassurance for shareholders, however. If investors as a whole decide that the transaction does not add value to the enlarged business, the share price may still fall even though earnings per share have not been diluted.

Directors' dealing

See INSIDER DEALING.

Discount rate

There are two meanings.

1 The rate of interest used to express a stream of future income in today's money values. The rate used should rise as the riskiness of the income stream actually materialising grows. It is intuitively obvious that $1,000 to be received in a year's time will be less valuable than $1,000 received today. But the question arises: what exactly will it be worth? Assume a nice-and-easy discount rate of 10%; on that basis, it is also intuitive that the answer is going to be about $900. In fact it is $909, because what we really ask is: what value today will produce $1,000 in a year's time assuming a 10% interest rate? Then we work back from there and divide $1,000 by 1.1, which is the result of compounding a unit at 10% for one year.

   Textbooks talk about a "discount factor" by which a future sum is multiplied to get a present value. This is simply the discount rate expressed in another way. It is the reciprocal of the compounding factor. For example, a sum compounded at 10% a year for five years will be worth 1.61 times its original value (the compounding factor). The discount factor then would be one divided by 1.61; that is, 0.62.

2 The rate of interest at which some central banks lend money to the banking system.

Discounted cash flow

Companies need benchmark tests to assess whether or not to raise funds from the capital markets for projects of their own (or whether, indeed, their own surplus funds might be better employed in capital projects or returned to shareholders). For a given level of RISK in a putative project – which, admittedly, is rather subjectively assessed – companies can find a corresponding rate of return from the markets then apply it as a DISCOUNT RATE to the likely cash flow that should be generated from the project. This analysis essentially takes two forms: an INTERNAL RATE OF RETURN calculation or NET PRESENT VALUE, which is closely related to it.

Dividend

The periodic cash sum paid on a company security, be it an ORDINARY SHARE, PREFERENCE SHARE or some type of loan STOCK. Dividends on preference shares and loan stock are almost always for a fixed amount (although occasionally they are linked to an appropriate benchmark, say the rate of inflation). Dividends on ordinary shares are more variable because such shares represent the RISK capital in a business, which is entitled to RESIDUAL INCOME only after prior claims have been paid.

Dividend cover

The number of times that a company's EARNINGS per share cover its DIVIDEND per share. Investors generally regard a ratio of two or more as comfortable and anything below one and a half times as potentially risky. If the ratio sinks below one, the company is paying part of its dividend out of its retained surpluses from previous years. This is not necessarily as bad as it sounds, because dividends are paid in cash and net surpluses in the INCOME STATEMENT are not a measure of cash. So if a company generates lots of FREE CASH FLOW it may be able to pay a dividend even though book-keeping items on the income statement (for example, the need to make provisions for the falling value of assets it employs) are hitting its declared profits. However, companies can and do cut their dividends if the dividend cover gets too low.

Conventional wisdom says that this is a matter of last resort, but research has shown that companies, particularly the smaller ones, cut dividends more often than supposed. (See DIVIDEND PAY-OUT RATIO.)

Dividend discount model

A tool for valuing an ORDINARY SHARE which says that the value of the share equals the present value of all its future dividends. This is pretty uncontentious; in a sense the share's value must embrace such a flow of income. However, the model also provides a basis for comparing the price of shares in the market with their theoretical value and thus judging whether the shares are cheap or expensive.

Perhaps dividend discount models suffer from being too theoretical because they are little used in the real world – especially in the UK – even though their record, such as it is, seems quite impressive. The fact that they can become quite complex and that they depend on the quality of the estimates fed into them does not help their cause. They come in three forms:

1 **Base-level model.** This values shares in much the same way as bonds. Thus the assumption is that the company's DIVIDEND will remain the same forever. Consequently, the value of the shares is simply the dividend divided by the required rate of return. So if a company was expected to pay a dividend of 10p a year in perpetuity, an investor whose required rate of return was 10% would value the shares at 100p each, and one who required 12% would value them at 83p.

2 **Constant growth model.** This assumes that dividends will grow by the same proportion each year and, as such, is also a fairly simple calculation. It can be simplified to state that the shares' value is the next dividend divided by the required

annual rate of return minus the rate at which dividends are expected to grow. If a 10p dividend is expected to grow by 5% a year, then an investor requiring a 12% return would value the shares at 150p each. The formula is:

$$10(1.05) \div (0.12 - 0.05)$$
$$= 10.5 \div 0.07$$
$$= 150$$

However, because the equation is sensitive to changes in the variables on the bottom line, someone wanting a 15% rate of return would only pay 105p (10.5 divided by 0.1).

3 **Multiple growth model.** This version tries to mirror reality by assuming that any company's dividends usually grow at different rates as its business moves through phases of growth, stability and decline. Take the simplest version, a two-stage model where the first stage is for a period of high dividend growth, say for five years at 20% a year, and the second for growth at a lower rate sustainable in the long term, say 10%. Assume also that the company is already paying an annual dividend of 10p and that an investor's required rate of return is 15%. A basic CASH FLOW calculation discounted at 15% tells us that the present value of the first stage's dividends is 57p.

Next apply the workings of the constant growth model to the second stage. This means grossing up the value of a 25p dividend growing at 10% by 5%. The 25p figure is the result of the 10p starting dividend growing at 20% for five years. The detail of the sum is:

$$24.9(1.1) \div (0.15 - 0.10)$$
$$= 27.4 \div 0.05$$
$$= 548$$

However, the 548p valuation arrives five years into the

future. It has to be discounted to a present value at the investor's 15% required rate. This equals 272p. Therefore the overall value of the share would be 57p plus 272p, which is 329p.

Dividend pay-out ratio

The DIVIDEND that a company pays expressed as a fraction of its EARNINGS. So if in a financial year a company pays a 4p dividend having declared earnings of 8p, the ratio would be 0.5. It is the inverse of DIVIDEND COVER and is generally used in the United States to define the ability of a company to fund its dividends. It is also important for its use in the adaptation of the constant growth DIVIDEND DISCOUNT MODEL to explain the PRICE/EARNINGS RATIO.

Dividend yield

The DIVIDEND paid on a share expressed as a percentage of its market price. So if a company pays a dividend of 60 cents per share in respect of a financial year and its shares trade on a stock exchange at $25, the dividend yield would be 2.4%.

> *The prime purpose of a business corporation is to pay dividends to its owners.*
>
> Benjamin Graham and David Dodd, *Security Analysis*

Dollar cost averaging

A simple and effective investment plan which virtually ensures success, as long as stockmarkets rise in the long run, as they have done to date in the western world. Investors put a fixed sum into the market at regular intervals. Thus they will buy a bigger quantity of shares when the market is low than when it is high, and their average buying cost will always be less than the market level while the trend remains upwards. The caveat is that in order to beat the market indices, investors still have to select the right shares. However, nowadays regular saving plans offered by mutual funds and investment companies make dollar cost averaging simple while simultaneously spreading RISK across a portfolio of stocks.

Charles Dow

With Edward Jones, Charles Dow (1851–1902) founded the Dow Jones Company, which provides financial information. In 1884 he developed his first stockmarket index, a 12-STOCK index of railroad shares which went on to become the Dow Jones Transportation Average. The forerunner of the DOW JONES INDUSTRIAL AVERAGE first appeared in 1897. From 1900 until his death, Dow was the editor of *The Wall Street Journal* in whose editorials he outlined what was later to be called DOW THEORY.

Dow Jones Industrial Average

Probably the world's best-known stockmarket indicator, because of its longevity (it dates back to 1897 when CHARLES DOW produced the original 12-STOCK average) and its association with *The Wall Street Journal*, which is published by Dow Jones & Co.

The Dow is simply the arithmetical average of the prices of 30 leading US stocks and carries no weighting for the stockmarket value of its constituent companies. The effect of this is that the Dow's value is disproportionately affected by those constituents which have particularly high stock prices and, correspondingly, the influence of companies which have had stock splits declines. The inclusion of 30 of the grandest, but not necessarily most dynamic, companies in the United States means that the average is more stable than other measures of US stock values. Despite these limitations, the average is updated every minute while the NEW YORK STOCK EXCHANGE is trading and it continues to be the most widely used measure of the value of America Inc.

Dow theory

A theory whose original aim was to use US stockmarket indices to comment on the outlook for the economy. It evolved into a tool for predicting movements in the US stockmarket and reached its peak when it forecast the Wall Street Crash of 1929. Although some say it forecast the October Crash of 1987, it has since declined in importance to the extent that it has few adherents today. Nevertheless, all over the world stockmarket pundits use its concepts, usually unknowingly, to explain and predict stockmarket levels.

The theory is named after CHARLES DOW, although it probably owes more to William P. Hamilton, editor of *The Wall Street Journal* from 1908 to 1929. Essentially it says that stockmarket cycles divide into three phases:

- **Primary.** Major upward or downward movements in the market lasting usually for several years.
- **Secondary.** Movements which either reinforce the primary trend or, at defining moments, predict its demise.
- **Tertiary.** Day-to-day movements which have little significance.

The chief characteristic of a BULL market would be where both high and low points of successive secondary phases move in an upward trend, especially if this were accompanied by rising volumes of stocks traded. Thus the market would be sustained by its support levels and would break through its resistance levels. However, when the market falls through a support level and is unable to bounce beyond a previous resistance level, it signals that a BEAR market has begun.

This is fine in theory, but, despite the success of the Dow theory in predicting the 1929 crash and possibly the 1987 crash, studies have shown that buying and selling a portfolio representing the DOW JONES INDUSTRIAL AVERAGE according to Dow's signals would have been much less successful than a simple buy-and-hold strategy.

DTB

Short for DEUTSCHE TERMINBÖRSE.

Duration

Several factors, such as COUPON, TERM and the prevailing level of interest rates, determine the price of a BOND. Duration is the measure that draws together all three of these into one number which quantifies the sensitivity of a bond's price to changes in interest rates. It does this in several stages. First, it puts a present value on the cash flows – the payment of DIVIDENDS and principal – that will accrue to a bond over its remaining life. Second, it weights these adjusted cash flows according to what fraction of the bond's current price they comprise. Third, it multiplies each weighted cash flow by the number of years before it will be paid (a payment due in three years would be multiplied by three, and so on). Last, it adds up the totals derived from stage three.

The result – the duration – is a figure, measured in years, which says how long it will be before a bond's purchase price has been repaid in present value money. More important are the following implications:

- the higher the duration, the greater is the sensitivity of the bond price to interest rate changes;

- low coupon bonds have a longer duration, therefore they are more sensitive to interest rate changes;
- for bonds with the same coupon, the duration will be higher, and therefore the interest rate sensitivity greater, for those with a longer term to maturity;
- by modifying the calculation for duration it is possible to estimate by how much a bond's price will change for a given movement in interest rates.

Earnings

The proportion of a company's profits which belongs to the shareholders and, therefore, a key figure in many share valuation yardsticks. Because they are a key figure, earnings are subject to much accountancy fudging. They are generally expressed on a per share basis and are calculated by dividing a company's weighted average number of shares outstanding for an accounting period into its profits after deductions for taxation, profits belonging to outside shareholders (minorities), extraordinary items and dividends to preference shareholders. Earnings come in several formats:

- **Basic earnings.** The figure shown by the company in the regular results statements that it is required to make.
- **Underlying earnings.** The figure that is derived from basic earnings by adjusting for any one-off items. So, for example, the costs of closing a division may be excluded, as might the profits from selling surplus fixed ASSETS.
- **Economic earnings.** The earnings that a company could fully distribute to its shareholders without eroding the REAL value of capital employed in the business.
- **Fully diluted earnings.** Earnings that take account of the shares that are likely to be issued in the future, given the existence of WARRANTS, OPTIONS and CONVERTIBLE securities.

Earnings announcement

When companies report new EARNINGS figures (half-yearly in the UK and quarterly in the United States), their share prices should respond rapidly to any surprise element in the figures. However, various studies have shown that there is often a sufficient time lag between the announcement and the price catch-up for some investors to make higher returns than an efficient market should permit. As such, this is an anomaly that EFFICIENT MARKET HYPOTHESIS should not allow.

Earnings yield

A useful, but largely ignored, investment ratio. At its simplest, it is a company's EARNINGS per share expressed as a percentage of the share's market price. So if a share's earnings were 30p and the share price was 450p, the earnings yield would be 6.7%. In other words, it is the reciprocal of the PRICE/EARNINGS RATIO (that is, 1/PE × 100) and has faded in comparison with that ubiquitous investment measure. Yet its value is that it describes the return on an ORDINARY SHARE in a similar way that YIELD TO MATURITY describes the return on a BOND. It therefore helps comparisons between shares and bonds.

In the stockmarkets it is rare for the earnings yield on ordinary shares to be as much as the redemption yield on good-quality bonds. Technically, this is because the redemption value of a bond is specifically factored into its redemption yield, whereas the value of an ordinary share on disposal is implicit only in earnings yield. Additionally, and more importantly, the return on bonds is set by the terms of their issue, but the returns on shares depend on many factors, although – crucially – they are not as vulnerable to inflation as are bond returns owing to the ability of companies to reprice their products.

In comparing shares and bonds using earnings yield, it should therefore be clear that shares become increasingly attractive as their yield approaches the redemption yield on bonds. Indeed, Benjamin GRAHAM, who is labelled the founding father of investment analysis, regularly constructed successful quantitative portfolios of shares for which he sought shares whose earnings yield was twice the yield on best-quality bonds. To put a measure of safety into such portfolios, Graham also insisted that the shares of companies included had to have less debt than their NET WORTH.

EBITDA

Short for earnings before interest, taxes, depreciation and amortisation. EBITDA is basically the cash profits that a company generates before interest and tax and is, therefore, a measure of the company's cash-generating capability. In isolation it does not mean much. However, it is useful when compared with a company's interest costs when assessing the company's potential to fund its activities through cheap loan capital rather than expensive EQUITY. For a listed company, EBITDA can be divided into its stockmarket value. The resultant ratio of market value to cash profits can then be used as a cheapness/expensiveness guide to the company's share price.

ECN

See ELECTRONIC COMMUNICATION NETWORK.

Efficient frontier

The line on a chart which marks out the best combination of RISK and return available to investors in a particular market. The theory is that all rational investors would buy assets which lie on the efficient frontier. Such assets are said to "dominate" all others, which either have less return or carry more risk. Plotting the efficient frontier therefore becomes a key aim of PORTFOLIO THEORY. In portfolio theory, as originally formalised by Harry Markovitz in the 1950s, the efficient frontier is arc-shaped because, at the margins, investors could seek extra return only by assuming disproportionate amounts of risk or sacrificing marginal returns as the price of shedding risk.

However, refinements to Markovitz's theory introduced the concept of the RISK-FREE ASSET, which investors could freely buy or borrow. The effect of putting a risk-free asset into the picture is to create portfolios whose returns cannot be bettered by standard Markovitz theory for a given amount of risk. Mathematically this must be so since the risk-free asset has a STANDARD DEVIATION of zero and therefore has no effect on the equations that shape portfolio theory. Whether investors in practice can happily borrow unlimited amounts of funds at the risk-free rate is another matter.

The effect was to make the efficient frontier a straight line sloping upwards, known as the CAPITAL MARKET LINE. The only point at which it touches Markovitz's arced efficient frontier – in the textbooks always picked out as point *M* for market – is where an investor would choose to put all his capital into risky market investments. All other portfolios are some combination of risky market investments plus or minus the risk-free asset. This deduction has important effects for stockmarket investors because it implies that they should do no more than buy a basket of shares that replicates the market's movements, then lever the returns up or down by combining these with borrowing or lending at the risk-free rate. As such, it is an important stepping stone towards the EFFICIENT MARKET HYPOTHESIS.

As to the point on the efficient frontier where each investor would choose to pick his portfolio, that would depend on where his own INDIFFERENCE CURVE of risk and return made a tangent with the efficient frontier. The assumption is that investors will always want better than the market offers and the point of tangent is the least unacceptable trade-off of risk and return that each investor is prepared to take.

Efficient market hypothesis

Arguably, no investment theory has generated as much hot air as the efficient market hypothesis (EMH). This is perhaps not surprising since it is almost designed to put academics and investors into opposing camps: the academics arguing that, at its extreme, EMH renders useless all attempts to outperform the market consistently; the investors pointing to the success of various of their number in doing so. In a way there had to be an EMH. It is the natural consequence of CAPITAL MARKET THEORY, which says that excess returns for a given level of RISK are always arbitraged away, therefore returns are only what the market allows, therefore the market is efficient.

At its simplest, EMH says that security prices quickly and accurately reflect all the relevant information that might affect them. In saying this, it assumes that we are talking about stockmarkets which are sufficiently big and liquid that no single investor can influence prices and in which information moves rapidly and, in effect, at no cost. The information is made available by the army of investment analysts employed in the investment industry. However, this creates a paradox: the analysts exist only because they and their employers think that it is worthwhile to collect and disseminate information, therefore they must believe that the market is inefficient. Yet the effect of all these analysts is to make the market efficient. Which is right? Formally, EMH splits into three forms:

1 **Weak.** The base level form of EMH which says that security prices reflect accurately all the past price data. This might

seem an irrelevance, except that it undermines the basis for TECHNICAL ANALYSIS, which assumes that past price data can give profitable clues to future price movements. Tests of weak-form EMH have favoured the academics; or, at least, the failure of many studies to find patterns in security prices has put the onus on technical analysts to show that their particular methods have some validity.

2 **Semi-strong.** The next stage says that all published information, especially relevant financial data, is reflected in STOCK prices. This form of the theory questions the use of FUNDAMENTAL ANALYSIS: the dissection of company accounts, industry trends and so on by investment analysts. Its proof depends on various studies which examine whether excess returns can be achieved from using publicly available information. For example, do prices respond to factors such as changes in the money supply or accounting presentation? Under the latter heading, if the market is efficient, share prices should respond to accounting changes which actually affect the value of a corporation but ignore those changes which are merely presentational. The evidence is mixed. It seems that it is possible to generate excess returns from fundamental analysis, but it is extremely difficult to do so.

3 **Strong.** The most demanding form, which says that security prices reflect all information, both public and private. Thus even those who act on inside information cannot consistently profit by doing so. It is the easiest of the three to test for, by looking at the performance of those with the most privileged information sources: fund managers and corporate insiders. The record of fund managers undermines strong-form EMH because many studies in both the UK and the United States have shown that most retail funds – that is, mutual funds and investment companies – do not beat the market, and fewer still beat it after adjusting for the risk they

bear. Studies of corporate insiders (officers or directors of companies who have to report their share dealings to the regulatory authorities) show that they are much better at producing excess returns.

The conclusion must be that large stockmarkets, such as those in New York and London, are efficient most of the time, but not always. This assessment is borne out, on the one hand, by the difficulty that most professional investors have in generating excess returns consistently and, on the other, the familiar stockmarket anomalies which should not exist if there were complete efficiency: low P/E stock; SMALL CAP STOCK; the effect of EARNINGS ANNOUNCEMENTS.

“ *We must bring Wall Street to Main Street – and we must use the efficient, mass merchandising methods of the chain store to do it.*
Charles E. Merrill, co-founder of Merrill Lynch

Efficient portfolio

Within the context of PORTFOLIO THEORY, which seeks to define the trade-off between RISKS and returns on investments, this is a portfolio which produces the best possible return for a given level of risk, or which offers the least risk for a given return.

Electronic communication network

An alternative form of stockmarket to a stock exchange, where trades are arranged by a computer that instantaneously matches mirror-image buy and sell orders, while unmatched orders are generally available for subscribers to view. The advantages of an electronic communication network (ECN) over a conventional stock exchange are that the ECN offers lower transaction costs and longer hours of trading. Increasingly, however, it is difficult to distinguish an ECN from a stock exchange, or from some of the services that a stock exchange offers. This is, perhaps, not surprising since the first ECN was the OVER-THE-COUNTER quotation system NASDAQ, which was introduced in 1971 and went on to become the model for matched-order trading that many stock exchanges introduced. More recently, stock exchange operating companies have bought established ECNS. For example, NASDAQ itself bought INET – a merger of two ECNS – and the NEW YORK STOCK EXCHANGE bought Archipelago, which itself had merged with the Pacific Stock Exchange.

Elliot wave theory

The works of Ralph Elliot (1871–1948), a little-known accountant, provide great succour to eternal optimists, because his chief idea was that stockmarkets – or, more precisely, the DOW JONES INDUSTRIAL AVERAGE, about which he wrote – basically go up. The proviso is that, according to Elliot, markets go up in cycles of advance and retreat. To complicate the picture there are cycles within cycles within cycles and so on.

Elliot postulated a grand supercycle, lasting 150–200 years, within which there are five supercycles within which there are five cycles within which there are five primaries. It is not too clear where these cycles begin and end, but many students of TECHNICAL ANALYSIS agree that the revival of Wall Street in 1932 was the start of a supercycle and that the BULL market which began in 1975 was the start of a cycle. Analysis of these cycles is based on waves, there being five waves which carry the market up (in which the first, third and fifth are up-waves and the second and fourth corrections), followed by three waves which take it down (the second of which is a part reversal of the down trend). At the end of this eight-wave pattern the market is always higher than where it started.

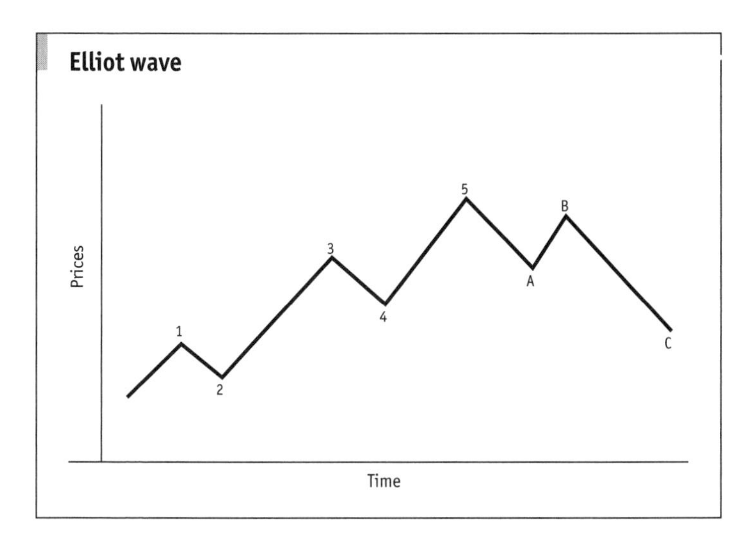

Taking its cue from DOW THEORY, Elliot analysis relies heavily on patterns of support for and resistance to particular market levels. It assumes that markets are powered by the psychology of investors whose optimism grows slowly, consolidates, gets out of hand, then bursts. As such, interpretation of market charts according to Elliot principles is more art than science. However, rigidly applying the principles of FIBONACCI NUMBERS to Elliot wave theory can produce detailed, but contentious, estimates of the values a market should move to.

Emerging market

An emerging market is the stock exchange for a country which has a low per-head income compared with the developed world and/or is not industrially developed, yet which has a functioning stock exchange, even if its standards hardly compare with those of North American and European exchanges. There may also be stringent controls on the inward and outward flow of investment capital. Thus most of the world's stockmarkets are emerging, as opposed to developed, but there is a grey area. For example, Hong Kong and Singapore both have high per-head incomes, but are sometimes still classed as emerging. Conversely, some countries in the former Soviet bloc are clearly industrialised (such as Poland and the Czech Republic), but the need to reconstruct their economies and build regulated stockmarkets means they are in the emerging category. Stockmarket indices provider FTSE International subdivides its classification into "developed", which includes Hong Kong and Singapore, "advanced emerging", which includes Brazil and Poland, "secondary emerging", which includes China and Russia, and "frontier", which includes Croatia, Nigeria and Vietnam.

The potential for emerging economies to produce rapid, albeit volatile, economic growth means that emerging-market investment funds have attracted much capital. However, their importance should not be overstated. They still account for just a few percentage points of the value of the world's stockmarkets.

EMH

See EFFICIENT MARKET HYPOTHESIS.

Enterprise value

A business's enterprise value is the stockmarket value of its EQUITY plus the value of the debt that it employs (some of which may also be quoted on a stock exchange). It is, therefore, a value of the total capital that the business uses. Enterprise value is used with EBITDA as a guide to the fairness of the company's valuation. Essentially, enterprise value divided by EBITDA is a ratio of business value to cash profits and can be a more useful touchstone than PRICE/EARNINGS RATIO, especially for companies that do not make much "accounting profit" (that is, profit after taking account of non-cash deductions such as AMORTISATION).

Equity

The high-risk capital that is committed to a business. It is high-risk because it has rights to the RESIDUAL INCOME and ASSETS of the business only after all other claims have been met. Thus decent amounts of equity capital are crucial to a risky venture which may not make profits for some years, if at all. In contrast, low-risk businesses need comparatively small amounts of equity and can finance themselves with higher levels of debt. This has driven the trend for some cash-generating companies to increase their borrowings and return large amounts of cash to shareholders through either buying in their shares or paying out big DIVIDENDS.

The major concomitant of the RISK that accompanies equity is that it brings ownership rights. In other words, owners of the equity own the business, even if for much of the time ownership is technical rather than real. (See also ORDINARY SHARE.)

Equity risk premium

The extra return that investors expect from putting their capital into equities rather than a RISK-FREE ASSET. In other words, it is the incentive that induces them to buy ordinary shares. So the risk premium is the hope, but not the guarantee, of a reward in the future. But the difficulty, as with so much in investment, is forecasting what it might be. Historically, the existence of an equity risk premium in the UK and US markets is not in doubt. It can be measured by subtracting returns on government bonds from returns on equities. So, for example, in the UK the equity risk premium over the past 80 years has averaged approaching 6% a year.

Within this period, however, there have been times of sustained poor performance by equities; for example, the early 1930s, early 1970s and the early 2000s when there was no reward for holding equities. So investors can have good reason to question whether there will be a reward for keeping equities during their holding period.

One solution is to estimate the future equity risk premium, and the simplest way to do this is to adapt the DIVIDEND DISCOUNT MODEL. Thus we can define the expected risk premium as the forecast DIVIDEND YIELD on equities plus the likely growth rate in dividends minus the redemption yield on government bonds whose maturity is the same as our holding period. This will provide an answer, although it will only be as good as the estimate in the growth rate for dividends, which in turn will be anchored to overall economic growth rates.

ETF

See EXCHANGE TRADED FUND.

Eurex

The name given to the FINANCIAL FUTURES exchange formed by the 1998 merger of Germany's DEUTSCHE TERMINBÖRSE and the Swiss DERIVATIVES exchange, Soffex. Each exchange continues to trade independently but they share a joint trading and clearing platform. Along with the NYSE, Euronext.LIFFE and the CHICAGO MERCANTILE EXCHANGE, Eurex is one of the world's "big three" derivatives exchanges.

Eurobond

The basic Eurobond is a FIXED-INCOME SECURITY which raises money for borrowers in a currency other than their own. It usually trades in bearer form and pays interest once a year without any deduction of tax. In addition, it accrues interest on the basis of a year comprising 12 30-day months. Most Eurobonds are listed on a recognised stock exchange – usually London or Luxembourg – although they trade OVER-THE-COUNTER.

Eurobond has also become a generic term for any BOND issued in the comparatively unregulated capital markets known as the EUROMARKET. It therefore includes bonds with exotic names, such as Samurai bond (technically a bond raised by a non-Japanese borrower in the Japanese market) or Bulldog bond (the same as a Samurai, but denominated in sterling and issued in the UK). The innovative nature of the Euromarket means that Eurobonds come in a variety of guises. For example:

- with WARRANTS, which may have a variety of functions. A killer warrant, for example, automatically calls for redemption of its host bond when it is exercised;
- with varying interest structures from ZERO-COUPON BONDS to floating-rate bonds, whose interest payments move with money market interest rates;
- with OPTIONS to redeem the bond on the initiative of either the borrower (CALL OPTION) or the investor (PUT OPTION), or no redemption at all (perpetual);
- with special repackaging. The Euromarket was largely responsible for creating the market in STRIPS. It created special securities by stripping coupons from US TREASURY BONDS, Australian government bonds – Dingos – and UK government gilts – Stags and Zebras.

Euromarket

The generic term for a vast OVER-THE-COUNTER market in promissory notes and BONDS centred in London. It grew up in the 1960s through banks arranging loans in currencies held outside their country of origin. Dollars were the favoured currency because they were plentiful and internationally acceptable, and tight capital-raising regulations in the United States persuaded borrowers to look elsewhere. Big US trade deficits mean the dollar remains the core Euromarket currency, but business is now done in all major currencies.

The Euromarket was primarily developed by leading European banks, but US and, in the late 1980s, Japanese banks have since become prominent. Although characterised by a lack of regulation compared with domestic stock exchanges, the Euromarket has its own regulatory organisation, the International Capital Market Association (ICMA), and two clearing operations, Cedel and Euroclear, which work with each other. It probably raises more capital than any other market except the US domestic bond market. In 2007 it raised $215 billion from the sale of FIXED-INCOME SECURITIES, which was 7% less than the amount raised in 2006. And at June 30th 2008 the ICMA estimated that the market value of bonds outstanding was almost $12 trillion.

Euronext

The name given to the merged cash and DERIVATIVES exchanges of Amsterdam, Brussels and Paris, which was formed in September 2000. Since then, Euronext has added BVLP, the Portuguese stock exchange, and, more significantly, the LONDON INTERNATIONAL FINANCIAL FUTURES AND OPTIONS EXCHANGE, which was taken over in early 2002. In April 2007, Euronext was taken over by the NEW YORK STOCK EXCHANGE, following a $10 billion cash-and-shares bid, to form NYSE EURONEXT.

Euronext.LIFFE

The derivatives arm of NYSE EURONEXT, which comprises the derivatives exchanges of the Paris, Amsterdam, Brussels and Lisbon stock exchanges and – biggest of all – LIFFE, formerly called the London Financial Futures and Options Exchange. LIFFE was acquired by Euronext for £555m in 2002 (and Euronext was subsequently taken over by the NEW YORK STOCK EXCHANGE in 2007). Within this grouping each financial FUTURES exchange continues to operate independently though they all use LIFFE'S CONNECT trading platform. Along with EUREX and the CHICAGO MERCANTILE EXCHANGE, LIFFE is one of the world's major derivatives exchanges. In 2007 it traded 949m contracts, an annual record and a 30% increase on 2006. Of these, 489m contracts were in interest rate products and 417m in EQUITIES and equity indices.

Ex-ante

The term used to denote the fact that an investment assessment has been made with historical data (literally "from before"). Most testing of PORTFOLIO THEORY is done with ex-ante data because they are plentiful and accurate, and therefore most appropriate for testing the sometimes complex mathematics involved. There is an irony, however, because any real investment is made on an expectation of the future. In these circumstances ex-post data ("from after") are more useful. The trouble is that ex-post data, by definition, are projected and thus less plentiful and possibly misleading. To the extent that the past often tells us something about the future, using ex-ante data is perfectly acceptable, but it does highlight a practical limitation of portfolio theory.

Ex-dividend

Stockmarket jargon indicating that the price of a share is quoted minus the entitlement to a DIVIDEND which has been recently declared but not yet paid. Other things being equal, the share price will fall by the amount of the payout the day the shares are declared ex-dividend. In both the UK and the United States dividends are paid to shareholders who are registered owners (holders of record), but in order to smooth administration for a company's registrar, whose responsibility it is to distribute the dividends, stock exchanges declare a share ex-dividend a few days before the registrar closes the share transfer book. (See also CUM-DIVIDEND.)

Ex-post

See EX-ANTE.

Ex-rights

When a company arranges a RIGHTS ISSUE, its existing shares trade ex-rights in the market when they no longer carry the entitlement to subscribe to their pro-rata entitlement to the new shares being issued.

Exchange traded fund

A cross between an ORDINARY SHARE and a MUTUAL FUND. Exchange traded funds (ETFS) are collective investment funds, most of which are designed to track a specified stockmarket index. Their shares are listed on stock exchanges and trade in the same way as shares in other listed companies. Although the share price of an ETF will respond to supply and demand (like company shares), it will not move far away from its underlying NET WORTH (unlike company shares). This is because the management firm that runs the ETF has the ability to swap ETF shares for baskets of the actual investments that the ETF owns and vice versa. This process – in effect continually adjusting the amount of ETF shares available to meet demand – exerts a strong influence on the ETF's share price.

Execution only

The no-frills, low-price share dealing service offered by a new generation of stockbrokers that has grown rapidly on the back of internet share dealing.

Exercise price

The price at which the right, but not the obligation, to convert an OPTION or a WARRANT into a security has been agreed. It is also known as the strike price.

Expected return

The investment return – in both DIVIDENDS paid and changes in capital values – that an investor expects from an ASSET over a specified period (usually one year). Because expected return looks to the future it can only be estimated, in contrast to realised return, which is the actual return over a past period. Estimating expected return is a key building block of PORTFOLIO THEORY, where returns are juxtaposed to RISK. Within portfolio theory it is calculated by taking all possible returns and weighting them by their probability of occurrence. Similarly, the expected return on a portfolio of investments is the weighted average of the expected returns for its individual components.

Fibonacci numbers

Named after their discoverer, a medieval Italian mathematician, Fibonacci numbers almost mystically crop up in all sorts of natural phenomena, from the way petals reproduce on a flower to the

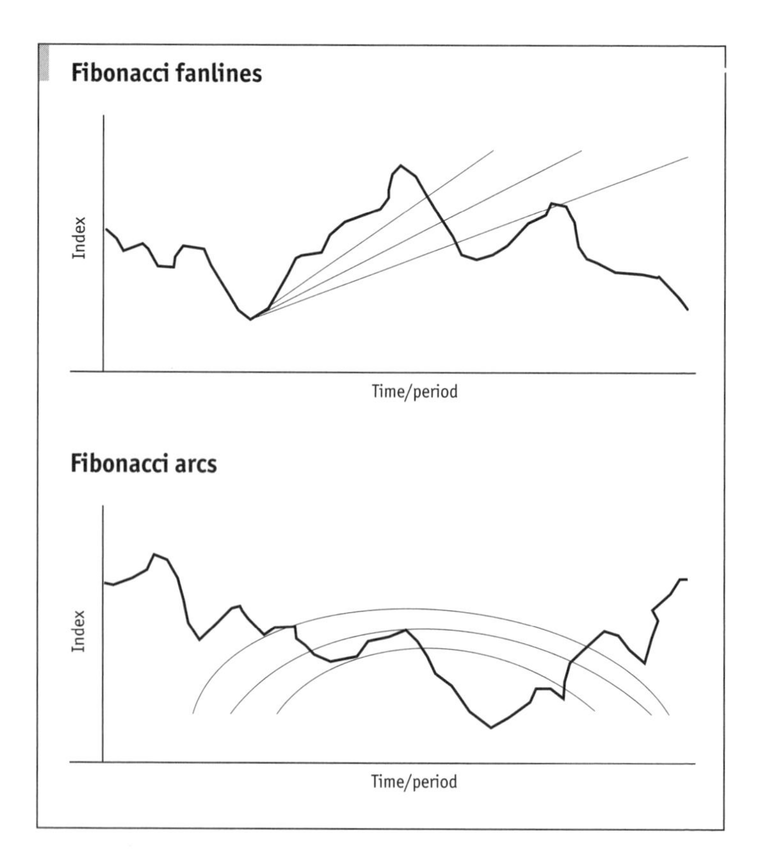

shape of a galaxy. That being so, why should they not help explain patterns of stockmarket movements? Fibonacci numbers are part of a sequence in which the next number is found by adding together the previous two in the series. Thus the sequence runs 1 1 2 3 5 8 13 21 and so on.

They have a ready application in ELLIOT WAVE THEORY because Elliot reckoned that each market cycle consisted of a five-wave up move followed by a three-wave down move, making eight in all. Keen devotees of the theory could then predict market tops and bottoms by using Fibonacci ratios, that is, the relationship between one Fibonacci number and its subsequent one. The most important of these are 0.6 (three divided by five) and 1.6 (five divided by three). To give an idea of the process, in a five-wave up move, the top of wave three might be estimated by taking the market level at the top of wave one, multiplying it by 1.6, subtracting the answer from the market level at the top of wave one and adding it to the market level at the bottom of wave two. Thus if the DOW JONES INDUSTRIAL AVERAGE were 4,000 and 2,800 at the end of waves one and two, this would forecast 5,200 for the top of wave three. The sum is ([4,000 × 1.6] − 4,000) + 2,800.

In practical terms, Elliot wavers would probably use various Fibonacci ratios to calculate fan lines on a chart which would spread out from a key market bottom, thus indicating future levels of support and resistance for the market.

FIFO

See FIRST IN, FIRST OUT.

Financial futures

Contracts traded on the world's FUTURES exchanges in claims of one sort or another on financial assets: currencies, interest rates,

BONDS or stockmarket indices. As with futures generally, they allow risks to be hedged or big bets to be placed on future price changes. Financial futures were born in 1972 when contracts in nine currencies were introduced on the CHICAGO MERCANTILE EXCHANGE. In 1975 interest rate futures began trading on the CHICAGO BOARD OF TRADE, and in 1982 the Kansas Board of Trade introduced the first stockmarket index futures contract when it began trading the VALUE LINE COMPOSITE INDEX. Since then products have proliferated. Almost all the world's major stockmarket indices have futures contracts traded either on divisions of commodity exchanges, such as the S&P 500 INDEX on the Chicago Mercantile Exchange, or on stock exchanges, such as the NYSE COMPOSITE INDEX, which is traded on a division of the NEW YORK STOCK EXCHANGE.

Financial Services Authority

The UK's chief regulatory body for the financial services industry. The Financial Services Authority (FSA) was established in 1997 when it took over supervision of the securities industry from the Securities and Investments Board. In 1998 supervision of the banking industry was added to its responsibilities, and it assumed its full powers following the assent of the Financial Services and Markets Act 2000. The FSA authorises and regulates all the firms and individuals working in the financial services industry, in both the professional markets (investment managers and STOCKBROKERS) and the consumer markets (building societies, friendly societies and financial advisers). Its aims are to maintain confidence in the UK's financial system, promote understanding of the system, protect consumers and reduce financial crime.

First in, first out

Commonly known by its acronym FIFO, a method of accounting for INVENTORY whereby the costs of the oldest stocks are deducted from revenues in computing profits. (See LAST IN, FIRST OUT.)

Fixed-income security

See next entry.

Fixed-interest security

A security on which the borrower agrees to pay regular fixed amounts of income (usually half yearly) and repay principal at a specific date. In the United States it is more generally known as a fixed-income security.

Flat yield

The YIELD on a BOND that is calculated simply by expressing its annual interest due as a percentage of its market price. So if a bond with a 10% COUPON trades at $112, its flat yield will be 8.9%. This information is of limited use since it takes no account of the fact that $12 of value will be lost over the remaining life of the bond, a factor which is, however, accounted for in the YIELD TO MATURITY (or redemption yield) calculation.

Floating-rate note

A type of BOND paying variable interest rates that are linked to rates in the wholesale money markets, usually the London interbank market but sometimes the market in US Treasury bills. There are variations, including the following:

- **Drop-lock bonds.** The interest rate floats until a specific event happens – usually interest rates hit a trigger point – which causes the interest rate to be fixed for the rest of the bond's life.
- **Flip-flop floating-rate notes.** A long-dated floating-rate note (FRN) can convert into a short-dated FRN and then, if the holder wishes, back into a long-dated security.

Forward price

The price at which a transaction, probably for a currency, will be settled on a specific date in the future. Note that the term "forward" means that the ASSET being exchanged will be delivered, in contrast to the FUTURES price, where the asset will probably not be delivered but offsetting arrangements will be made.

Frankfurt Stock Exchange

The biggest of Germany's eight regional stock exchanges whose history dates back to 1585 and which accounts for over 75% of securities trading in Germany. The Frankfurt Stock Exchange is effectively run by the DEUTSCHE BÖRSE, whose responsibility it is to ensure that the exchange's trading and settlement procedures are effective. There is computer trading of bigger stocks through its Xetra trading system as well as traditional floor trading.

Free cash flow

The cash generated by a company from its normal trading operations which is left over for the shareholders. In other words, it is the cash flow from operations less the prior claims needed to keep the business running in good order. Thus it includes deductions for capital spending as well as taxation and changes in working capital, but not DIVIDENDS paid on the ORDINARY SHARES. If the information is available, it is sensible to fine-tune capital spending to exclude the cost of projects that are intended to expand the business and simply focus on replacement expenditures.

FRN

See FLOATING-RATE NOTE.

FSA

See FINANCIAL SERVICES AUTHORITY.

FTSE AIM Indices

A series of three indices launched in 2006 that give product providers the opportunity to offer – and investors the opportunity to buy – tradable products, such as EXCHANGE TRADED FUNDS, in baskets of AIM (Alternative Investment Market) shares. The three indices are the FTSE AIM UK 50 Index, comprising shares in the 50 largest AIM-traded companies measured by the stockmarket value of their equity; the FTSE AIM UK 100 Index, comprising shares in the 100 largest AIM-traded companies; and the FTSE AIM All-Share Index, which, at October 30th 2008, was an average of shares in 1,118 AIM-traded companies.

FTSE All-Share Index

The most widely used broad indicator of London share values. Often called simply the All-Share Index, as at September 30th 2008 it comprised 669 shares representing over 90% of the market value of shares listed in London. It dates back to 1962 and, therefore, has a long price history. It is an arithmetical index of the price of its components weighted by their stockmarket value, thus providing a more suitable base for comparing portfolio performance than an unweighted index would. Additionally, the index is broken down into ten sectors and 38 subsectors of industry, providing useful benchmarks for the share price performance of individual companies.

> *Not to bet until the odds be considered fair, reasonable or completely in the favour of the backer is an advantage which must never be surrendered. The bookmaker has to lay odds all the time for each and every race – but the backer can choose if and when to bet.*
> *Braddocks Complete Guide to Horse Race Selection and Betting*

FTSE 100

Now the best-known indicator of share values on the London stockmarket, even though it only started in January 1984. The index, generally referred to as the Footsie, comprises shares of 100 of the largest companies by stockmarket value listed in London. Its constitutents are reviewed quarterly, when a company's share will be included in the index if its market value ranking has risen to 90th or better. Simultaneously, those shares whose ranking has fallen to 111th or below will be removed from the index. It is an arithmetic index weighted by market value, which means that the impact of price changes of the larger companies is proportionately greater than the smaller ones, thus, theoretically, mimicking the portfolios of big institutional investors. Its launch was driven by the need for London to have a suitable price index against which contracts could be written in the OPTIONS and FUTURES markets. Hence its base value of 1,000, a figure sufficiently large to ensure that every day the index should move by whole numbers. Its price is continuously updated during the LONDON STOCK EXCHANGE'S trading hours.

FTSE 250

The London stockmarket index for shares in the 250 listed companies whose market values rank immediately below those of the FTSE 100. Because of the rules for inclusion and exclusion in the FTSE UK indices, there is some blurring at the margins. To move from the FTSE 250 to the FTSE 100, a company's market value would have to be 90th or better at the time of the quarterly review of constituents. To be relegated from the FTSE 250, a company's value would have to be 376th or below. Because its components lie mid-way between the biggest and smallest of London's listed companies, it is also known as the Mid-Cap index. Like the FTSE 100, it is an arithmetic index weighted by market value.

FTSE 350

A stockmarket index for the combined components of the FTSE 100 and FTSE 250 indices.

Fundamental analysis

On the assumption that a security has a true value, which might differ from its stockmarket value, it is the job of fundamental analysis to estimate what that true value may be. To do this, investment analysts will look at the fundamentals of the security concerned: what is likely to be the present value of the future CASH FLOW that an investor will get from the security? If it is an ORDINARY SHARE, on what multiple of EARNINGS should it trade? In turn, this requires detailed work on the status of the issuer of the security and the economic variables that will affect it. Looked at another way, fundamental analysis is everything that TECHNICAL ANALYSIS is not.

Futures

Futures transfer RISK from those who do not want it to those who do. Investors with portfolios of shares who fear that the market will fall can sell their shares, but it would be a costly way of shedding risk. Alternatively, they can agree to sell a contract in a stock-market index, say, three months in the future at its current level plus an adjustment for the interest costs they bear for carrying their portfolio. If the market falls, as expected, the profit investors make from selling their futures contracts above the then current index level will cancel out, or at least reduce, the losses they sustain on the portfolio.

A futures contract is, therefore, a standardised forward contract. In other words, two parties agree to trade an ASSET at a point in the future. But because the trade is off-the-peg rather than bespoke, the asset being traded is precisely specified, as is the quantity traded, the settlement date for the trade and the minimum amount by which the contract price can vary. This degree of standardisation is possible because trading is conducted through a recognised exchange and comparatively few contract specifications are authorised. This has two main advantages:

1. As all trades are made with the exchange's clearing operation, the risk that the party on the other side of the transaction can default is effectively eliminated, thus generating confidence in the market.

2. Authorising only specific contracts concentrates trading in those areas, thus supplying the liquidity – the ease of buying and selling with low TRANSACTION COSTS – on which all markets thrive.

(See FINANCIAL FUTURES.)

“ *Sometimes your best investments are the ones you don't make.*
Donald Trump, American businessman

Futures option

The development of markets in both OPTIONS and FUTURES probably meant it was only a matter of time before the two came together. They did so in the early 1980s with the introduction of options in a range of futures in currencies, interest rates, share indices and commodities. A futures option acts much like a normal option, except what is being traded is the right (but not the obligation) to be a buyer or seller of a futures contract, which is, itself, a deferred purchase or sale. As such it might seem pretty pointless, but futures options do offer scope to speculate on a futures market without being subject to MARGIN calls if the price of the futures contract moves away from the option holder.

GAAP

See GENERALLY ACCEPTED ACCOUNTING PRINCIPLES.

Gann theory

As with the other main theories of TECHNICAL ANALYSIS – DOW THEORY and ELLIOT WAVE THEORY – Gann theory puts much emphasis on finding levels of support for and resistance to price changes in financial markets. However, unlike CHARLES DOW and Ralph Elliot, W.D. Gann was a successful trader in both stocks and commodities. He was also a mathematician who, like Elliot, believed that universal principles controlled the movement of markets.

The more exotic elements of Gann theory concern so-called cardinal squares. The theory's most widely used application, however, is in emphasising the relationship between price changes and time. The basic building block of this is a trend line on a chart that ascends at 45 degrees from the start price at the left-hand end of the chart. Thus the trend line plots one unit of price change for one unit of time. If actual price changes rise faster than this, the investment is in a BULL phase and vice versa. Other support/resistance lines can then be plotted on top of this showing faster/slower price changes.

Gearing

The term used in the UK to measure the proportion of debt held by a company in relation to the funds belonging to shareholders. Thus a company which had, say, total net debt of £200m and shareholders' funds of £400m would have gearing of 50% (see LEVERAGE).

Generally accepted accounting principles

The broad and often detailed guidelines which suggest, and sometimes dictate, how companies should draw up their accounts. The term has a special meaning in the United States because there the SECURITIES AND EXCHANGE COMMISSION (SEC) has statutory power to ensure that companies whose STOCK is traded publicly draw up their accounts according to generally accepted accounting principles (GAAP). Indeed, in 2002 the SEC's power was strengthened by the SARBANES-OXLEY ACT, which created a Public Company Accounting Oversight Board whose function is to regulate the accounting firms which audit (and verify) company accounts.

Geometric mean

In investment terms, this is the compound rate of return required to turn an initial sum into a closing sum given a specific number of compounding periods. An initial investment of $1,000 which became $2,000 after five years would have a geometric mean (compound growth rate) of almost 15% per year. Arithmetically it is defined as the *n*th root of the product that results from multiplying a series of numbers together where *n* is the number of numbers in the series.

Within investment, which devotes much attention to

considering returns over particular periods of time, the geometric mean is used more often than the ARITHMETIC MEAN. However, there are occasions when using the arithmetic mean is better. Take the series below, which shows year-end values and annual returns on the DOW JONES INDUSTRIAL AVERAGE of US stocks.

Say we wanted to think about the future and answer the question: what is likely to be the return from the Dow this year? Based on past results, the correct figure to take would be the arithmetic mean because this shows the average return in any one year. However, if we wanted to know the average growth rate that took the Dow from 8,342 to 13,264 over the five years from end-2002 to end-2007, then the geometric mean would be the one.

Note that unless the numbers in the series all change by the same rate, the geometric mean will always be less than the arithmetic mean; and the difference between the arithmetic and geometric means will widen as the variability of the series increases.

	Year-end	*Return (%)*
2002	8,342	...
2003	10,454	25.3
2004	10,783	3.2
2005	10,718	–0.6
2006	12,463	16.3
2007	13,264	6.4
Average returns		
Arithmetic mean	10.2%	
Geometric mean	9.7%	

Gilt-edged stock

Or simply gilts. The name for BONDS issued by the UK government to fund its debt; so called because the likelihood of default on either interest payments or principal was (and is) effectively zero. As at September 2008 there were £497 billion of gilts outstanding, comprising 76% of the UK government's debt. Of these stocks, £144 billion were in INDEX-LINKED GILTS and almost all of the remainder in conventional fixed-interest stocks.

Glass-Steagall Act

A 1933 act of the US Congress which separated commercial banking – that is, taking deposits and lending on the funds at a MARGIN – from INVESTMENT BANKING – that is, underwriting securities issues and investing in equities. The effect was to split up the banking empire of J.P. Morgan into Morgan Guaranty Trust and Morgan Stanley. A Financial Modernisation Act in 1999 finally led to the dismantling of Glass-Steagall restrictions just as further scandal rocked the investment banking industry.

Golden cross

Moving averages move technical analysts, and rarely more so than when they form a golden cross on a price chart, or its bearish

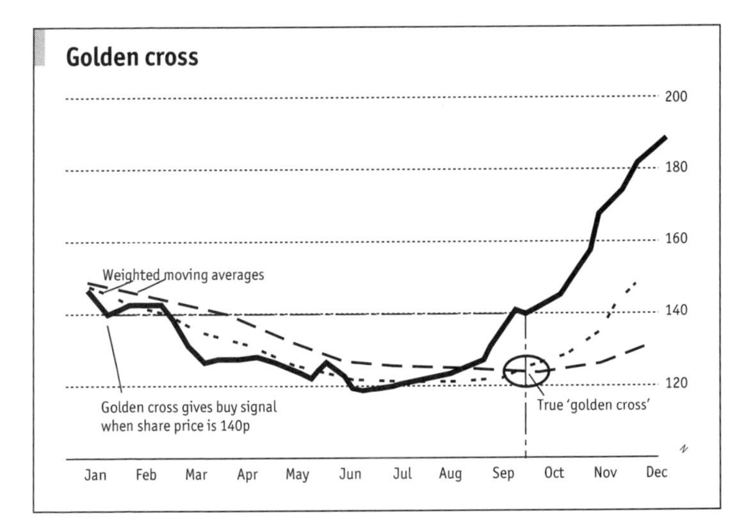

opposite, a DEAD CROSS. A golden cross is where a short moving average (say, the rolling average of 20 days) breaks above a longer moving average (say, 50 days). The signal will be so much the stronger if the cross is formed after the moving averages have stayed close to each other for some time, since this indicates a shift in the market's perception of the STOCK in question and a willingness to take it to new higher ground.

Goodwill

That indefinable something that makes a business special. Because it is indefinable it cannot be separated from the rest of the company's ASSETS and therefore cannot be included in its BALANCE SHEET as part of its NET WORTH. However, it can be included if it is goodwill which has been acquired when buying another business, where it is defined as the excess over fair value paid for the acquired business. Fair value is the value of the acquired business's net assets adjusted for differences in the accounting policies between the two companies. In general, companies in both the United States and the EU no longer amortise their goodwill as a cost against profits but subject it to a so-called "impairment test" every year and make write-downs if necessary.

The effect of including or excluding goodwill from balance sheets is the same as including or excluding INTANGIBLE ASSETS, and the debate about the merits of doing either generates the same amount of hot air. For investors who want to assess the value of a business, the sensible course is generally to include acquired goodwill in the balance sheet as this gives a better idea of how much capital has been used to generate its profits.

> *The different systems – Ben Graham, growth stocks – are fine, as long as you have the discipline to stick to them ... Myself, I have no system. I'm a pragmatist. I just wait until the fourth year, when the business cycle bottoms, and buy whatever is offered.*
>
> Larry Tisch, from *The Money Masters*

Graham, Benjamin

Often referred to as the "Dean of Security Analysts", Benjamin Graham (1894–1976) more than anyone gave formal structure to the process of investment analysis. He did this by rigorous analysis of the financial statements of corporations as detailed in SECURITY ANALYSIS, which he co-wrote with David Dodd and which, over 70 years after publication, remains an important text. His more accessible book, *The Intelligent Investor*, deals more with the psychology of investing and has been in print continuously since it was published in 1949. Graham was a successful investor in his own right and funds managed by his business, Graham-Newman Corporation, grew by 21% a year between 1936 and 1957. His teachings are synonymous with VALUE INVESTING and he is, perhaps, best known as the mentor of Warren BUFFETT.

Greenmail

A form of blackmail practised by one company on another, primarily in the United States where the rough and tumble of takeover bids is more aggressive than in Europe.

One company builds up a substantial shareholding in another, then threatens either to mount a full-scale bid or to sell its stake to another potential bidder unless the management of the company under threat agrees to buy out the shareholder for a substantial profit. Managements counter the threat of greenmail by putting in place POISON PILL plans.

Grey market

The trading that takes place between the launch of a new share issue and the delivery of allotment letters, which tell applicants how many shares they have received. Such trading is, therefore, done at RISK because sellers do not know how many shares they have and buyers may not know the price at which the shares have been allotted. This did not stop sometimes active grey markets developing, especially in shares of utilities privatised by the UK government. Grey markets, in effect, are encouraged by the LONDON STOCK EXCHANGE, as it begins its official dealings before allotment letters have been delivered.

Hang Seng Index

The main stockmarket index for Hong Kong. It comprises shares in 42 blue-chip companies and is computed as the ARITHMETIC MEAN of their price changes weighted by their market capitalisations. It was launched in 1969 but has been backdated to July 1964 and a base value of 100. During trading the index's value is calculated every 15 seconds.

Head and shoulders

Among the patterns that technical analysts search their charts for, head and shoulders patterns are among the best known and, with

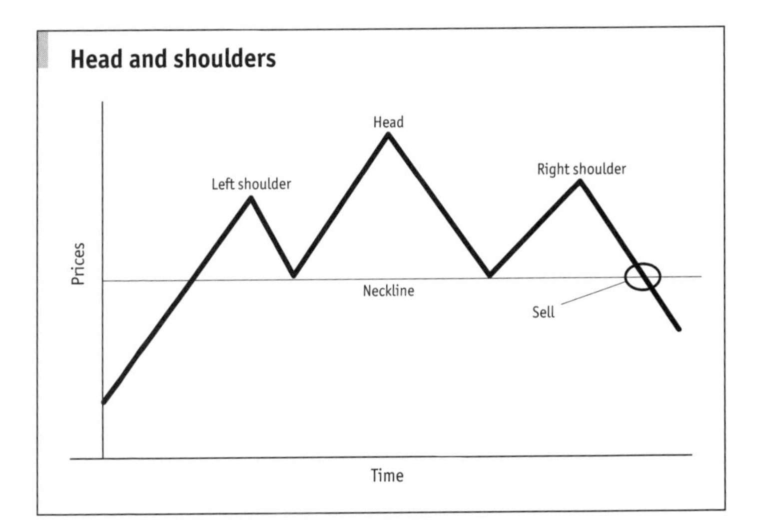

hindsight, can be applied to some of the great stockmarket crashes of history, from the SOUTH SEA BUBBLE of 1720 to the October crash of 1987. The idea is that following a sustained run-up in the price of a STOCK (or a market) the price reaches a new high based on heavy volume of trading then subsides (the left shoulder). This is followed by another surge to a new high, but probably based on lighter volume (the head). Following another correction the price surges again but on much lighter volume and fails to reach its previous high (the right shoulder). If the price then falls below the neckline – that is, the line which underpins the previous lows formed in both shoulders – this would be taken as a strong sell signal.

Hedge

To hedge is to remove RISK from a transaction that will take place some time in the future. Thus, in the standard explanation, a commodity producer will agree to sell its goods at a specific price on a specific date in the future, and a commodity processor will agree to buy them. The two parties have nullified the risks they each faced: the producer the possibility of having to sell in a falling market; and the processor the risk of having to buy in a rising market.

The idea carries over into the financial markets. The equivalent of the commodity producer is an investor with a portfolio. The investor is LONG of stocks, and in selling an appropriate number of contracts in the FUTURES of a STOCK index effectively protects the value of his portfolio against an overall fall in the value of stocks. The equivalent of the commodity processor is someone who is prepared to go long of stocks some time in the future, probably a SPECULATOR or an investor who needs to unwind an earlier hedge.

Hedge fund

There is no specific definition of a hedge fund. According to a report by the US finance industry's regulators into the collapse of a high-profile hedge fund in 1998, a hedge fund is "any pooled investment vehicle that is privately organised, administered by professional investment managers and not widely available to the general public". Conspicuous by its absence in this definition is any reference to hedging, the activity that gave these funds their name. To HEDGE is to insure against loss, and the original aim of a hedge fund, as defined by Alfred Jones, an American financial journalist who is widely credited with creating the first hedge fund in 1949, was to insure a portfolio of investments against losses by simultaneously holding both LONG and SHORT positions. In other words, regardless of the movements in the financial markets to which the fund was exposed, some of its ASSETS would rise in value and some would fall. Thus overall returns to the fund itself would be protected – that is, hedged – and, hopefully, would always be positive, though that would depend on the skill or luck of the fund's manager (not that any fund manager ever admitted to good luck).

However, as hedge funds reached what may well prove to be their high-water mark in 2006–07, increasingly they came to be defined by how they behaved. In particular, hedge funds would be characterised by high management fees, extensive use of LEVERAGE and highly correlated investment returns.

Typically, a hedge fund charges a flat annual management fee of, say, 2% of the fund's asset value and a performance fee, which often starts at 20% of a fund's profit within an accounting period (that is, the increase in its asset value from the start to the end of the period). In contrast, a MUTUAL FUND normally charges its investors no more than 1.5% a year with no performance fee. With such high fees available, it is small wonder that hedge funds proliferated. Using leverage magnifies funds' returns – both profits and losses – and accounts for much of the hugely successful performance of some funds during BULL markets. However, as the report cited above noted, with a little understatement, the use of leverage by many funds "can make them somewhat fragile institutions that are vulnerable to liquidity shocks". Given that, it may be noteworthy that hedge funds as a group have so far emerged from the CREDIT CRUNCH looking less battered than other institutions – in particular, the commercial and investment banks whose proprietary trading desks have similar characteristics to a hedge fund.

However, a concern is that increasing evidence shows that, in a BEAR market, hedge funds cease to perform a hedging function. This may be because too many of them have similar investment plans, often using illiquid assets that are both difficult to value and difficult to trade. As a result, their returns are highly correlated (that is, they tend to move in the same direction). The trouble is that this rather defeats the point of putting capital into a hedge fund in the first place, since a time of falling markets is precisely when an investor looks to hedge funds to add the value that conventional investments almost by definition cannot.

Hedge ratio

Options can insure a portfolio of shares as well as being speculative, and the hedge ratio, which predicts how much an OPTION's price will move for a given change in the price of the underlying shares, defines how much exposure to options is likely to be needed to hedge a position in ordinary shares perfectly. The ratio is derived from the BLACK-SCHOLES OPTION PRICING MODEL and holds good to the extent that the future VOLATILITY of the share price echoes its past.

Assume, for example, that an investor has a holding of 5,000 shares in a company, that the standard US arrangement of 100 shares per options contract applies and that a hedge ratio for call options in the shares is 0.6. To hedge his position fully, the investor will need to write (that is, sell) 83 call options: $5{,}000 \div (0.6 \times 100)$.

Horizon premium

The excess return that investors seek for holding comparatively risky long-term BONDS as opposed to comparatively safe short-term bonds, or Treasury bills. Over the long term in the United States this premium has been about 1.5 percentage points, although interestingly it has been rather less in the UK, where inflation (and therefore short-term interest rates) has been consistently higher. It can, therefore, be used as a cheapness or expensiveness indicator for long-term bonds.

IFRS

See INTERNATIONAL FINANCIAL REPORTING STANDARDS.

Immunisation

The investment strategy for protecting a BOND portfolio against the risk of rising interest rates. Theoretically, this is possible because of the twin effects of rising rates. They depress the price of bonds, but they raise yields, therefore allowing future income to be reinvested at higher rates than previously expected. A bond portfolio would be immunised if its DURATION equalled the investor's expected investment period. However, this is more theoretical than real because the portfolio would have to be continually rebalanced so that its duration matched the investment period.

In the money

Assume we are dealing with a CALL OPTION, which gives the holder the right to buy a share, then the OPTION contract will be in the money if the market price of the underlying shares is greater than the price at which the option holder can exercise his rights. Say a share trades at 430p, then an option to buy that share at 400p will be 30p in the money. Another way of putting this is that it has 30p of INTRINSIC VALUE because anyone would pay at least 30p to acquire this option.

Note that for PUT OPTIONS the opposite is the case. A put

option is in the money when the market price of the share is less than the price at which the option holder can sell the share.

> *Our merchants and master manufacturers complain much of the bad effects of high wages in raising the price, and thereby lessening the sale of their goods both at home and abroad. They say nothing concerning the bad effects of high profits. They are silent with regard to the pernicious effects of their own gains. They complain only of those of other people.*
>
> Adam Smith, *The Wealth of Nations*

Income statement

That part of a company's financial accounts showing the following:

- How much revenue was generated in a particular year.
- What costs were incurred in order to produce that revenue.
- What profits (surpluses) or losses (deficits) were left.
- How much taxation was charged on the profits.
- How much profit was left over for the shareholders.

Most important to grasp is that the income statement (formerly the profit and loss account) is not just about the cash going in and out of the business. Rather, it is based on the ACCRUALS CONCEPT: that income and costs should be matched as far as possible with the period when they occur, not when the cash moved in or out. Thus some non-cash charges are regularly levied on the income statement. Most significant are DEPRECIATION and the provision for taxes that will have to be paid in the future.

Correspondingly, some cash costs are not charged to the income statement when they are incurred, especially the cost of STOCK unsold at the end of the year and expenses deemed to be part of the capital cost of an ASSET in the making. Notable under this heading would be interest incurred on the borrowings for plant and buildings under construction, or the development costs of a major new product. Such expenses are often capitalised in the BALANCE SHEET. Reconciliation of these items with the company's underlying cash position should be made in the CASH FLOW statement. Nevertheless, good investment analysis demands that the accounting treatment of such items be critically assessed. In particular, changing policies for depreciation and capitalising costs can result in exaggerated profits. Similarly, big one-off items that occur in one year's income statement should be stripped out and, if possible, averaged out over the years to which they really relate.

Index arbitrage

A particular type of PROGRAM TRADING which, according to some, was largely responsible for the spectacular fall in share values on Wall Street in October 1987.

Index arbitrage essentially works by taking advantage of any anomalies that occur between the value of a basket of stocks which can replicate a STOCK index – say the S&P 500 INDEX – and the value of an OPTIONS or FUTURES contract in that index. If the basket of stocks is expensive compared with the index futures, traders will sell the stocks and buy the futures, or vice versa, until any worthwhile profits opportunity has been priced away. This is easier said than done because the basket of stocks has to be bought or sold quickly, and this requires sharp organisation.

The trouble most often arises on the day when the options or futures contracts expire. This causes the value of the contracts and the value of the stocks used as a substitute for the index to align, as they must (otherwise there would be no profits for those who have successfully hedged). This can cause massive trading, buying or selling, in the underlying securities and consequently rapid movements in the market indices.

> *Investors should understand that what is good for the croupier is not good for the customer. A hyperactive stockmarket is the pickpocket of enterprise.*
>
> Warren Buffett, chairman, Berkshire Hathaway

Index fund

The inability of most professional fund managers consistently to beat the returns on major stockmarkets led to the growth of index funds. Known as tracker funds in the UK, they are portfolios constructed so that their returns mirror as closely as possible those of a chosen index, most commonly the S&P 500 INDEX in the United States and the FTSE ALL-SHARE INDEX in the UK. This is achieved by either holding every share in an index in line with its market-value weighting within the index or, more likely, holding a basket of shares whose total returns have matched the index in the recent past and so, the assumption goes, are likely to do so in the future. By adopting this low-key approach such funds expect to save on running costs which, in itself, will be an important factor in ensuring that returns match the index more closely. Thus, predictably, a MUTUAL FUND that aims to track an index will include low charges as part of its marketing pitch.

Index-linked gilts

UK government securities whose principal and interest payments are tied to the Retail Prices Index (RPI), the most widely used measure of inflation in the UK. Index-linked gilts were first issued in 1981 in response to widespread demand from investing institutions during a period of sustained high inflation in the UK. In theory, they allow institutions with long-term LIABILITIES, which can be closely defined, to match their assets to those liabilities. They have never been especially popular, however, perhaps because their returns have rarely compared with those consistently generated by risky equities.

Furthermore, the index-linking they offer is selective. First, because the RPI may be an inadequate benchmark for some investors (pension funds, for example, may prefer to link their liabilities to the rise in wages, not prices). Second, an index-linked gilt is not actually linked to the change in inflation during its life. Rather, it is tied to the level of RPI eight months before it was issued until eight months before it is redeemed. The need to be able to calculate the value of both dividends and redemption within a reasonable time made such an adjustment almost inevitable. However, it does mean that investors holding an index-linked gilt to maturity face some residual RISK, which may work for them or against them.

Index-linked security

Any security whose redemption value and dividends are tied to an index, most probably the changes in a relevant stock exchange index or the security's domestic rate of inflation. Best known are INDEX-LINKED GILTS, although in the UK several investment trusts have issued stocks which are tied to a stockmarket index. In the 1970s the French government issued a BOND which was linked to the price of gold. From the borrower's point of view it was a disaster.

Index option

By far the most popular form of OPTION, the index option allows investors to speculate on movements in stock exchange indices or to insure their portfolios against unfavourable changes in STOCK values. Index options for most major indices are available nowadays; for example, the S&P 500 INDEX, the NYSE COMPOSITE

INDEX, the NASDAQ 100 Index and others on various US exchanges (although the Chicago Board Options Exchange dominates); the FTSE 100 Index in London; the CAC 40 INDEX in Paris; and the DAX 30 in Frankfurt.

The major difference between index options and stock options is that settlement is always for cash, whereas stock can be delivered as settlement with stock options. Effectively, therefore, traders in index options pay and receive a unit price per point of the underlying index; $100 per point on the S&P 500 Index, for example, and £10 per point on the FTSE 100. So if, say, the S&P 500 closed at 850, then someone with a CALL OPTION on the index with a STRIKE PRICE of 845 could exercise the option and make a gross profit of five times $100.

In addition, note that options on the S&P 500 are European-style options which do not allow early exercise. In London's EURONEXT.LIFFE market investors get a choice between European-style and American-style options on the FTSE 100; options on the CAC 40 are American-style.

Indifference curve

A concept from the theory of consumer demand which has an application in PORTFOLIO THEORY. On a chart the curve shows all the combinations of two things to which a consumer is indifferent; that is, the consumer will accept the combination of the two offered at any point on the curve. In portfolio theory the two variables are RISK and return. So the curve illustrates the degree of risk that an investor will assume for a given reward, and vice versa. When juxtaposed with the risk or reward trade-off that a market actually offers, the point at which the investor's indifference curve makes a tangent with the line of the market risk or return (known as the EFFICIENT FRONTIER) is where the investor would choose his portfolio.

Individual retirement account

A US savings plan to shelter retirement income from tax. As at 2008, contributions of up to $5,000 per person per year are allowed with an additional $1,000 a year for those aged over 50. One type of individual retirement account (IRA) permits contributions regardless of income, whereas another type, a Roth IRA, has an income limit set each year by Congress. Eligible investments are a wide range of STOCKS, BONDS and managed funds.

Individual savings account

The UK government's tax-free savings vehicle that replaced the PERSONAL EQUITY PLAN and the TAX EXEMPT SPECIAL SAVINGS ACCOUNT in April 1999. Savers are allowed to put a wide range of investments into an individual savings account (ISA), including shares in EU companies that are listed on a recognised stock exchange, UNIT TRUSTS, investment trusts and to a lesser extent cash. All capital gains and income received on ASSETS held in an ISA are tax free. However, cash withdrawn from an ISA cannot be returned except as a fresh subscription up to the permitted maximum amounts. For 2008–09 these were £7,200 overall including £7,200 for shares and £3,600 for cash.

Initial public offering

When shares in a company are offered to outside investors for the first time and simultaneously the company arranges to have its shares listed for trading on a recognised stock exchange. Usually, though not necessarily, in an initial public offering (IPO) the company raises new capital for its own uses and some of the existing shareholders sell some of their holdings.

Avoid "inside information" as you would the plague.

Philip L. Carret, from *The Art of Speculation* (1930)

Insider dealing

There are two distinct and different meanings.

1 Illegal dealings in securities (most often purchases) by people with confidential information which they use for their own gain or that of associates. The archetypal case is of someone in the corporate finance department of a STOCKBROKER or an investment bank who knows that a company will shortly be in receipt of a bid from another and buys shares in the target company to profit from any jump in the share price that follows the announcement of the bid. Practices such as this are illegal in all major financial centres, although they remain notoriously difficult to prove and convictions are few and far between.

2 The purchase or sale of shares in a company by its directors during periods when it is perfectly proper for them to deal. The practice is watched closely on the basis that a company's directors know more about it than any outside observers and therefore their actions are a good guide to its prospects. Directors' sales may not be so important. They may sell shares for any number of reasons. However, purchases by clusters of directors where they put a significant amount of new money into their company's shares (that is, the shares are not purchased solely through the exercise of options awarded as part of their remuneration packages) can often be a useful indicator of good things in store for a company. In the UK it is more often known as "directors' dealings".

Intangible assets

The process of valuing and deciding whether to include or exclude intangible ASSETS from a company's BALANCE SHEET is a wonderfully grey area for accountants and therefore a source of confusion for investors. Basically, intangibles are assets without a physical form (they are not plant and equipment), which are separately identifiable from a company's other assets and to which a stream of revenue can be attributed. Patents, copyrights and franchises are typical intangibles. More controversially, in the UK brand names which have been acquired are also intangibles, but brands which have been built up are rarely classified as such.

Classification of what comprises intangible assets and how they are accounted for matters because it affects both the NET WORTH of a company and its EARNINGS. Including intangibles on the face of the balance sheet increases the net worth, but their value has to be depreciated and this reduces earnings. Excluding them – that is, writing off their value against the capital reserves of the business – is good for earnings but not for net worth. Often companies get round this difficulty by including intangibles on their balance sheet but, rather than depreciating them annually, they subject the intangibles to an annual impairment review. (See also GOODWILL.)

Internal rate of return

The DISCOUNT RATE which, when applied to a series of future cash flows, would make their present value net out at zero; that is, the present value of the cash received from an investment would be the same as the present value of acquiring that cash. As such, the internal rate of return (IRR) is used to test investment opportunities against a benchmark rate of return. If the IRR on an opportunity is likely to be higher than the benchmark, the investment is viable; if not, forget it.

The IRR cannot be solved directly but has to be found by trial and error. If an investment's cash flows produced a value of -$2,000 over its life when a 15% discount rate was used and a value of $10,000 with a 10% discount rate, common sense says that the IRR will be nearer to 15% than 10%. This is simply because -$2,000 is closer to zero than $10,000. How much closer is defined by the difference between the discount rates chosen and the gap between the valuations they produce. In this case the difference between discount rates is 5 percentage points and the gap between the values they generate is $12,000, that is, $10,000 – (-$2,000). Thus the IRR will be ten-twelfths of the gap between 10% and 15%. The sum is:

$$\text{IRR} = 10\% + [(10 \div 12) \times 5\%] = 14.2\%$$

Doing a calculation such as this long-hand is time consuming. Happily, however, financial calculators and computer spreadsheets invariably have the ability to do the iterative process quickly and accurately. (See YIELD TO MATURITY.)

I've worked myself up from nothing to a state of extreme poverty.
Groucho Marx

International Financial Reporting Standards

These are the rules that outline the principles – as well as much of the detail – upon which companies must report their financial performance. International Financial Reporting Standards (IFRS) are the standard reporting rules for companies within the European Union whose shares are listed on a recognised stock exchange. In the United States, the aim is that the GENERALLY ACCEPTED ACCOUNTING PRINCIPLES issued by the Financial Accounting Standards Board should converge with IFRS.

IFRS are issued by the London-based International Accounting

Standards Board. Many of the board's older statements are known as International Accounting Standards (IAS). From 1973 to 2001 the board issued IAS; since 2001 it has issued IFRS. Entities that prepare accounts according to IFRS rules must produce: a BALANCE SHEET; an INCOME STATEMENT; either a statement of changes in equity or a statement of recognised income or expense; a CASH FLOW statement; notes to the accounts.

Intrinsic value

An expression that has a specific meaning and ones of increasing vagueness:

- The specific definition applies to OPTIONS and WARRANTS in which the intrinsic value is what an investor must pay for the right to buy or sell a share at some point in the future. So if the price of a share were 150p and there was an option to buy it at 120p, someone must be prepared to pay 30p for that privilege. Thus the intrinsic value is defined as the share price minus the EXERCISE PRICE, assuming the result is positive.
- More vague, the intrinsic value of an investment is all the cash that it will ever generate expressed in current monetary values. In a sense this must be so; all it is saying is that a share is worth no more than it is worth. The difficulty lies in finding what that value is. In investment analysis, for example, the intrinsic value of a company is often defined as all the future FREE CASH FLOW discounted to present value. This is fine in theory, but forecasting all those cash flows is impossible and the correcting mechanism of adding a RISK premium into the chosen DISCOUNT RATE to allow for all those unknown factors falters because of its subjectivity.
- So vague as to be useless, sometimes it is argued that some objects, usually gold, have intrinsic value regardless of their

market price. This claim is most likely to be trotted out by people with a vested, not to say desperate, interest in seeing the market price move in their favour.

Inventory

The goods and materials that a company holds to sell to a customer in their finished form. Therefore, inventory – formerly called stock in the UK – consists of raw materials, work in progress and finished goods. Included in these may be the labour costs needed to bring the goods to their finished state.

Investment banking

This is a bit of a misnomer. It is the type of banking associated with firms such as Morgan Stanley, Goldman Sachs and Credit Suisse First Boston and which, arguably, is not banking at all. Its roots lie in the separation of deposit-taking banking from banking involving the underwriting of securities offerings. This division was forced in the United States by the 1933 GLASS-STEAGALL ACT, which was passed in response to the speculative excesses of some banks in the 1920s, which were exposed by the 1929 stockmarket crash.

Nowadays investment banking is synonymous with the financial conglomerates which conduct a full range of investment-related activities from advising clients on securities issues, acquisitions and disposals of businesses, arranging and underwriting new securities issues, distributing the securities and running a fund management arm. The growing presence in investment banking of European and Japanese banks not limited by US banking laws and the effective dismantling of the Glass-Steagall Act mean that the division between investment and commercial banking is increasingly artificial.

Investment trust

See CLOSED-END FUND.

IPO

See INITIAL PUBLIC OFFERING.

IRA

See INDIVIDUAL RETIREMENT ACCOUNT.

IRR

See INTERNAL RATE OF RETURN.

ISA

See INDIVIDUAL SAVINGS ACCOUNT.

January effect

January is different from other months in the stockmarket. A study of market returns in 16 countries found that in 15 of them January produced above-average returns and that this effect is strongest in the UK and the United States. For example, a study of US STOCK returns for 1904–74 showed that the average monthly return was 0.5%, but for January it was 3.5%. Furthermore, in the United States the feature is concentrated on the stock of small corporations. The DOW JONES INDUSTRIAL AVERAGE of 30 leading corporations showed no January effect. This could be for tax reasons, because stocks are sold towards the end of the tax year in December, then bought back at the start of the new tax year. As the UK's tax year runs till the end of March this does not explain why the UK has a January effect; despite this, for small British companies January is the worst month of the year. The fact that both stocks which pay no dividends and those with a high YIELD also do well supports the notion that January's excess returns are essentially a catch-up exercise. The odd thing is that this phenomenon persists even though it is so well known.

Japanese candlestick chart

So called because each entry looks like a candlestick and the charts originated in 19th-century Japan, where they were used to follow the rice market. These charts are a sophisticated version of charts which show the high, low and closing price of a marketable investment. The fact that they come from the mysterious east and have exotic names to describe some of their formations – hanging

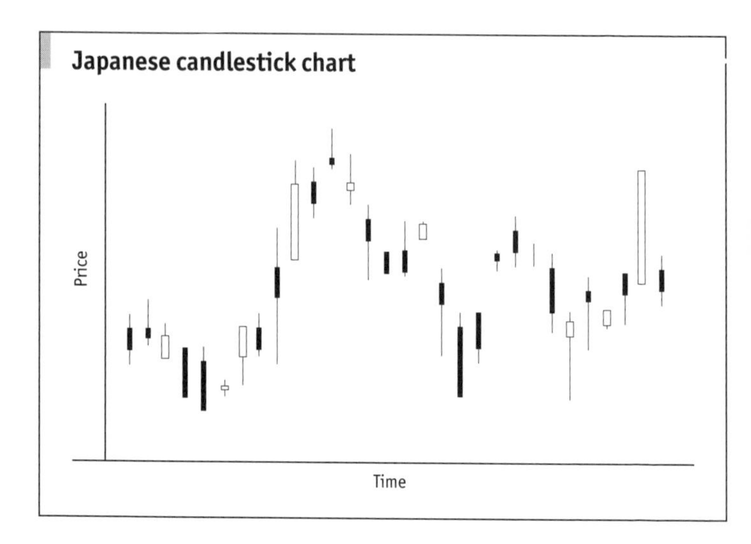

man, dark cloud cover, *doji* – adds to their attraction. More importantly, they pack a lot of information into a small space.

Junk bond

A type of security that took corporate America by storm in the 1980s. Strictly speaking, junk bonds are FIXED-INCOME SECURITIES that fail to make investment grade; for example, they are below grade BB according to Standard & Poor's BOND RATING. Many of them became junk bonds by being "fallen angels"; they started out as investment grade, but fell. However, in the 1980s an OVER-THE-COUNTER market in junk bonds was underwritten primarily by STOCKBROKER Drexel Burnham Lambert specifically to fund corporate deals (mergers, takeovers, restructurings). The justification for this was that junk bonds were far less risky than was thought and therefore the excess yields they offered easily compensated investors for the extra RISK involved in holding them. Their success was phenomenal. The par value of junk bonds outstanding rose from $15 billion in 1980 to over $200 billion in 1989.

However, default rates rose too, reaching 9% of the par value of bonds outstanding in 1991. That was the year that Michael Milken, the driving force behind Drexel's domination of the junk market, entered prison for a ten-year sentence (subsequently reduced) after pleading guilty to charges of felony, bribery and racketeering relating to junk securities. Drexel had filed for bankruptcy the year before.

“ *Debt isn't good and it isn't bad.*

Michael Milken

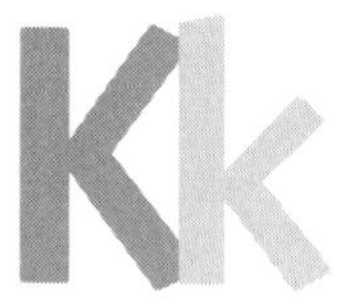

Keogh plan

A US tax shelter for self-employed people saving for their retirement. As at 2008, someone who is self-employed can put 20% of their income up to a maximum $46,000 into a Keogh plan. Contributions are tax deductible, although proceeds cannot be withdrawn without penal tax rates until the plan member is 59½ or becomes disabled. Common STOCKS, BONDS and MUTUAL FUNDS are all eligible for inclusion in the plan and the income accrues tax free until it is withdrawn.

Kondratieff cycle

A long-term cycle in economic activity identified by Nikolai Kondratieff, a Russian economist. By studying the economies of the UK, the United States and France, Kondratieff suggested cycles of 48–54 years' duration which were driven by long-term demands for capital and sustained, for a while anyway, by the rising wealth that the capital investment created. Subsequent work on his ideas suggests that his cycles peaked in 1812, 1866, 1920 and 1974.

Last in, first out

How a company accounts for its INVENTORY has a big effect on the profits it declares and the taxes it pays. The United States is unusual because its tax authorities are among the few that allow companies to account for their inventory on the basis of last in, first out (LIFO). This means that the inventory whose cost is first of all deducted from revenues for computing profits is that which was most recently purchased. Assuming that the cost of inventory rises, then the effect is to minimise both declared profits and tax payable. It is logical in so far as it excludes profits which are simply the result of the fortuitous gain in the value of inventory and it shows profits in a conservative light. In those industries where the cost of raw materials often falls (notably some branches of the electronics industry) it is equally logical to apply FIFO costings to inventory, and this does happen. The aim for investors, however, is to establish which method of inventory calculation a company is using – by no means easy given the variations available – and adjust for consistency with comparator companies. Analysts of US corporations are helped by reporting regulations that require corporations using LIFO accounting to show comparable FIFO figures.

Leverage

One of the wonders of capitalism, but always a potential horror, too: the means by which investment returns are enhanced through using fixed costs which have first call on a stream of income or a fund of capital. Leverage (better known as GEARING in the UK) pervades all investment-related areas:

Operational. All companies use leverage in their everyday operations because many of their costs are fixed or, at least, sticky (that is, they rise with extra business activity, but not much). Thus marginal income becomes particularly valuable because a high proportion of it feeds straight through to profits.

Financial. Companies add to their leverage through their financial structure because, for the most part, the cost of debt and preference shares is fixed. Thus once the obligations on these have been covered, extra revenues belong either to the ordinary shareholders or to the tax man. It is within the context of companies' financial structure that the term is most often used. Hence highly LEVERAGED BUY-OUT, a practice common since the mid-1980s, where a business's managers substitute much of the firm's EQUITY with debt in order to enhance returns on the shares of which they are likely to be substantial holders.

Investment. Like a company's, investors' returns can be improved by borrowing. Clearly, if the cost of debt is, say, 12% a year and investment returns are 15%, then all the excess returns on that portion of a portfolio funded by debt belong to the investors, raising the average return on their own capital. Some canny investors even manage to borrow money without cost. For example, insurance companies have the free use of a pool of money paid to them by policyholders, which they can invest until it is needed to meet claims.

Exotic leverage. Some companies have complicated capital structures in which several layers of shareholders have rights to income or capital, with each successive group in the pecking order having a more leveraged exposure to remaining funds. These are usually CLOSED-END FUNDS where, for example, the first call on distributable income may go to preference shareholders. First call on capital may belong to zero-coupon preference shares whose return depends on getting a lump sum when the company is liquidated. Remaining income and capital might then go to ordinary shareholders, whose investment would necessarily be a risky one.

Leveraged buy-out

Shorthand for the practice of buying a company using lots of debt finance and comparatively little EQUITY. For the buyers, which are increasingly PRIVATE EQUITY firms, the attraction is fatter investment returns, though obviously these come with greater RISK of failure.

Starting in the 1950s in the United States, leveraged buy-outs had moved into mainstream finance by the 1980s when corporate raiders used LEVERAGE to acquire companies whose performance was poor and whose management was wasteful. The type of business that attracted predators would probably have low levels of debt, predictable cash flows from which new debt could be serviced, tangible ASSETS such as real estate that could be used as collateral for debt, and the potential to make comparatively simple operational improvements.

Leveraged buy-outs are feasible because in most countries, including the United States and the UK, interest on debt is deductible against taxes. In effect, this makes debt finance cheap compared with equity, and it creates an additional stream of income – the taxes saved as a result of the tax deductibility – that accrues to owners of the equity.

Liability

Something that is owed. In the context of company accounting, it is the BALANCE SHEET value of a future obligation. Put another way, a liability is the mirror image of an ASSET. But, like an asset, measuring its actual amount is often easier said than done. Many of a business's liabilities are simple to quantify. A bank loan for £1m would be recorded as £1m plus however much interest had accrued at the date that the borrower makes up its books. Other transactions are not so straightforward. Say that a business receives £1m from a customer in return for an obligation to provide services in the future. The £1m cash received goes straight to the assets side of the business's balance sheet as a cash deposit, but how should it record its liability? If the business is confident that it can perform its services at a cost of £0.5m, that amount might be all the liability that it needs to show and the other £0.5m could go straight into the INCOME STATEMENT. If it were less sure about the cost of its future obligation, it might record the other £0.5m in the balance sheet as deferred income, or something similarly vague. If it were ultra cautious, it could treat the full £1m as a liability. Issues such as these matter to investors because different companies record such transactions differently, making harder the investor's job of doing intercompany comparisons.

LIFO

See LAST IN, FIRST OUT.

> *Tips! How people want tips! They crave not only to get them, but to give them. There is greed and there is vanity.*
>
> Edwin Lefevre, *Reminiscences of a Stock Operator*

Livermore, Jesse

One of the great speculators in US STOCKS and commodities in the first third of the 20th century, Jesse Livermore (1887–1949) made his greatest killing when he sold stock SHORT ahead of the Wall Street Crash of 1929. By 1931 his fortune was estimated at $31m, but by 1934 he had lost it all and filed for bankruptcy, his life ruined by the discovery that his alcoholic wife was having an affair with a prohibition agent. In 1949 he killed himself in the men's room in New York's Sherry-Netherland Hotel. Nowadays he is best remembered via the fictionalised account of the early part of his career in Edwin Lefevre's *Reminiscences of a Stock Operator*, which, over 80 years after it was first published, remains in print and widely read.

London International Financial Futures and Options Exchange

In its eventful 25-year history, the London International Financial Futures and Options Exchange (LIFFE) came close to becoming the world's biggest FINANCIAL FUTURES market, suffered from competition with EUREX and was taken over by EURONEXT in 2002. It opened for trading in 1982 and merged with the London Traded Options Market in 1992, then with the London Commodity Exchange in 1996, before swapping its mutual status for that of a shareholder-owned company and accepting Euronext's £555m offer.

London Stock Exchange

Still, by a small margin, Europe's biggest stock exchange measured by the number of companies whose shares are traded on the exchange and the market value of the equity of those companies. At the end of September 2008, shares in 3,183 companies were admitted to trading on either the main market or the secondary market, the ALTERNATIVE INVESTMENT MARKET (AIM), with a market value of £3,294 billion. Of these, 1,087 were domestic companies whose shares were fully listed and had a combined market value of £1,264 billion. Shares in 1,596 companies were traded on the AIM, with a market value of £45 billion. The remainder were major international companies whose shares were listed in London as well as – for the most part – their own domestic stock exchange. In contrast, Europe's second biggest stock exchange is EURONEXT, which is an amalgamation of the exchanges of Paris, Amsterdam, Brussels and Lisbon and had a market value of £1,250 billion.

Its history dates back to 1773 when stock brokers and stock jobbers (wholesalers) moved out of Jonathan's coffee house in the City of London into their own premises nearby. In 1986 it underwent BIG BANG, its most fundamental reorganisation. At that time it introduced a screen-based trading system, SEAQ, closely modelled on that of NASDAQ. In 1997 it replaced the use of competing MARKETMAKERS to drive equity trading in bigger stocks with a MATCHED BARGAIN system, and in 1999 it lost many of its regulatory responsibilities to the FINANCIAL SERVICES AUTHORITY. In 2001 it missed the opportunity to acquire London's FUTURES exchange and still lacks a DERIVATIVES arm. The same year it became a public company and its shares were listed on its own stock exchange. In 2007 it took over Italy's stock exchange, Borsa Italiana.

“ *Henry, why do people who have enough money try to get more money?*
Ruth Wilcox to Henry Wilcox in E.M. Forster's *Howards End*

Long

A term generally applied to those taking speculative positions in a market, or those whose job it is to supply a market with liquidity (MARKETMAKERS in London, specialists in New York). Thus if traders are long of STOCK they hold the stock in question and consequently may be vulnerable to sellers appearing in numbers (see SHORT).

Long-only fund

An investment fund whose success depends on the rising values of the ASSETS that it owns or has OPTIONS to buy. As such, a long-only fund is the opposite of a HEDGE FUND and, until the astounding growth of hedge funds early in the 21st century, no one had felt the need to apply the qualification "long-only" to funds that were the norm.

Low price/earnings ratio stock

One of the stockmarket anomalies that seems to produce consistently high returns: that investing in a portfolio of diversified stocks which have a low PRICE/EARNINGS RATIO (P/E ratio) will generate better returns than the market average or a similar portfolio of high P/E ratio stocks. Evidence for this has been found in many studies in both the UK and the United States. The excess returns may have been concentrated in stocks with small market capitalisations, although studies to adjust for this "size effect" have produced mixed findings. It is clear, however, that the excess returns have not been a product of assuming greater RISK. If anything the reverse is true: a portfolio of low P/E ratio stocks will have less risk (as measured by STANDARD DEVIATION or BETA) than a high P/E ratio portfolio. The best explanation of this anomaly, therefore, is that investors generally underestimate the potential for earnings recovery from low P/E ratio stocks and overestimate potential future growth from those with high P/E ratios. To the extent that profits growth in companies is random – that is, unforeseen factors cropping up mean that few companies can grow their earnings at a consistent rate year in, year out – this is a logical conclusion. (See EFFICIENT MARKET HYPOTHESIS.)

Mm

Marché à Terme des Instruments Financiers

The Paris market in FINANCIAL FUTURES, which is part of EURONEXT. The Marché à Terme des Instruments Financiers (MATIF) was founded in 1986 and trades contracts on a screen-based system, which replaced its trading floor in 1998.

Marché des Options Négociables de Paris

Paris's TRADED OPTION market, founded in 1987, which trades options by both OPEN OUTCRY and a computer-assisted order book. The Marché des Options Négociables de Paris (MONEP) offers contracts on the CAC 40 INDEX of leading French companies, as well as options in the shares of over 80 major companies.

Margin

Not the same as PROFIT MARGIN, this is the deposit or collateral that a trader must post with the party on the other side of a transaction – the counterparty – to cover the risk of loss that his counterparty carries. The need for margin arises because the trader has borrowed to buy whatever is the ASSET in question, or has sold the asset SHORT or has entered into a FUTURES contract.

When a trader deals on margin he is using LEVERAGE, which will magnify his profits but do the same to his losses – hence the need for security against possible losses. Margin can be in the form of securities as well as cash.

Should the price of, say, an ORDINARY SHARE fall below the level where an additional deposit was needed, the trader's counterparty – either his broker or the exchange on which he has traded – would issue a margin call. At that point the trader could either post additional margin and continue to run his position or liquidate it.

Mark to market

Basically, the daily adjustment to the value of an investment trading account to reflect changes in the market prices of components of the account. The term is most often used in FUTURES trading, although it applies equally when someone deals in cash securities using partly borrowed money. If the market value of the ASSETS pledged to the account falls beyond a certain level, the trader will have to make further pledges. In the futures markets trading accounts are marked to market every day, sometimes within a day's trading if price movements are especially volatile. Traders then have to make good any MARGIN commitments before the start of the following day's trading or face liquidation of the account.

Marketmaker

A stock exchange trader whose prime role is to continuously make markets in designated securities – that is, stand ready to buy and sell them regardless of market conditions, though only at prices and in quantities that the marketmaker specifies. As such, the marketmaker provides the market with liquidity.

At the NEW YORK STOCK EXCHANGE, the only major stock exchange that combines a trading floor with an electronic order book, "designated marketmakers" have taken on the role previously done by specialists. Thus the designated marketmaker in each STOCK – and no security has more than one marketmaker – functions as a broker and matches buy and sell orders when trading conditions permit. When order matching is not possible, the marketmakers have an obligation to maintain an orderly market in their securities and so buy and sell stock as principal.

At the LONDON STOCK EXCHANGE, marketmakers took over the function of stock jobbers, which existed until BIG BANG in 1986, though their role has been marginalised since London's STOCK EXCHANGE TRADING SERVICE became established. However, in a small number of securities stock is still supplied by marketmakers competing against each other to offer the best price and size. In such securities – those traded under London's SETSqx and SEAQ systems – there must be a minimum of two marketmakers.

Matched bargain

A trading system in which a stockmarket's trading platform matches buyers and sellers who are willing to deal in a security at the same price. In contrast, in a MARKETMAKER trading system specialised dealers act as wholesalers between buyers and sellers. The chief advantage of a matched bargain system is that it cuts dealing costs by eliminating the wholesaler's turn, but its shortcoming is that without the input of marketmakers, who theoretically stand ready to deal whatever the circumstances, market liquidity can dry up in extreme conditions. Despite this, throughout the world's stock exchanges matched bargain trading is gaining at the expense of marketmaking, especially in the shares of the biggest companies.

MATIF

See MARCHE A TERME DES INSTRUMENTS FINANCIERS.

Merger accounting

UK terminology for POOLING OF INTERESTS accounting when two companies are put together.

Mezzanine finance

Various types of finance which, in terms of RISK AND REWARD, bridge the gap between EQUITY and bank debt in the financing of a business. Mezzanine finance was developed in the United States in the 1960s, but received a big boost in the 1980s as the number of business deals using lots of LEVERAGE expanded rapidly. The aim of using mezzanine capital to finance a venture is to reduce the overall cost of capital while keeping the ownership rights tightly held. However, mezzanine finance often comes with an "equity kicker". This might take the form of WARRANTS attached to loans or simply loans which are convertible into ORDINARY SHARES. Alternatively, straight loans may have a kicker which gives them extra interest if the business's profits cross a threshold.

Modigliani-Miller theorem

A theory that explains why a company's financial structure matters. In so doing, it provides an intellectual basis for much of the corporate finance activity that has shaken up the business world of developed economies for the past 25 years. It is named after two American economists, Franco Modigliani and Merton Miller (1923–2000), who have both received the Nobel Prize in Economics for their contribution to financial theory.

The basic theory, which was published in 1958, explains that in a world where there is no taxation, no variation in borrowing costs between borrowers and no information anomalies there would be no difference between the value of a company that was wholly financed by EQUITY and one that was funded by a combination of debt and equity.

To see why, imagine two investment propositions: you could buy either a company that was financed wholly by equity, or one that was funded by a combination of debt and equity. Clearly you would have the option to buy the company that was funded solely by equity and borrow the same amount as the one that was partly funded by debt in order to finance your purchase. But, if you did so, your returns would be the same as the returns from the company financed by both debt and equity. If the returns from the two propositions are the same, their value must also be the same.

However, in the real world there are asymmetries, such as different tax treatments between equity and debt and varying borrowing costs for different borrowers. In these circumstances capital structure does matter. In particular, there are advantages for firms to substitute debt for equity because interest payments on debt are tax deductible whereas DIVIDEND payments are not. In effect, therefore, the taxes saved by raising debt become an ANNUITY payment that belongs to the owners of the firm's equity. Hence the fashion, from the 1980s onwards, for company bosses to raise debt and narrow the equity base of their companies – a practice that has been taken to the extreme by the PRIVATE EQUITY industry.

Momentum

In investment there is the notion of RANDOM WALK, which says that STOCK prices have no memory and, therefore, recent price changes have no significance. In contrast, there is also the notion of momentum, which effectively says that they do, so recent price changes have meaning. In other words, momentum investing is about buying stocks that have recently been showing strength on the assumption that whatever factors are causing them to rise will continue to have influence for a while. Research has shown that shares do indeed have momentum, so, for example, buying a basket of the best performing stocks over a period just ended will on average produce excess returns for a forthcoming period. After allowing for the lack of liquidity of some stocks and for dealing costs, the results are much less clear cut. However, momentum investing is taken sufficiently seriously for Value Line, a US investment service, and Company REFS, a UK service, to rank shares on the basis of their recent price momentum.

MONEP

See MARCHE DES OPTIONS NEGOCIABLES DE PARIS.

Money market fund

A MUTUAL FUND which puts its capital into short-term money market ASSETS, such as bank certificates of deposit, Treasury bills and commercial bills. In so doing, money market funds generate higher interest returns than bank savings accounts, from which they suck deposits. First introduced in the United States in the early 1970s, when interest rates were particularly high, money market funds have been successful at attracting money. Savings in them were $3,743 billion at the end of 2008, according to the Investment Company Institute.

Mortgage

The legal agreement in which one party (the mortgagee) agrees to make a loan and in return for which the borrower (mortgagor) agrees to pledge specific ASSETS as security against the loan.

Mutual fund

Also known as an open-end fund and in the UK as a UNIT TRUST. Mutual funds are pooled funds, mostly investing in ORDINARY SHARES, whose success in attracting capital to manage has been notable. In the United States the amount of money invested in equity mutual funds rose from $495 billion at the end of 1985 to over $6,000 billion by the end of 2008; a compound annual growth rate of 12% during a period when the value of US stockmarkets, as measured by the S&P 500 INDEX, compounded annually at 9%. In addition, at the end of 2007 there was about $5,500 billion invested in other types of mutual funds, most of which invested in a mix of EQUITIES and BONDS. The main characteristics of mutual funds are as follows:

- There is no secondary market in the shares (units) of a mutual fund. Someone who wants to invest in a mutual fund does so by buying new shares in the fund, which consequently expands in size. Conversely, investors can only sell shares back to the fund, which shrinks when this happens. Hence the term "open end".
- These transactions take place at the per share value of the fund's investments less various administrative charges. This is feasible because in general mutual funds hold marketable securities which can be readily valued as they trade on a recognised stock exchange. It gives a mutual fund an important edge over a CLOSED-END FUND, whose shares usually trade at less than their net asset value.
- Mutual funds are typically formed by a firm that specialises in investment management. The founding firm appoints a board of trustees to look after the interests of the shareholders (known as unit holders in the UK). In particular, the trustees appoint a management company to run the fund's investments. Most often it is the firm that launched the

fund in the first place. The managers are remunerated by fees charged on new units when sold (the "load" fee) and by annual fees charged against the fund's income or capital.

- By investing in many securities, mutual funds can spread their risk. This is particularly important for small investors, who may not have the resources to buy a diversified portfolio themselves. The rules under which they operate, however, limit this goal because if they want to keep their tax benefits, mutual funds must remain fairly fully invested in their chosen medium. In the United States, for example, mutual funds must earn at least 90% of their income from holding securities. Consequently, they may be particularly vulnerable to falling stockmarkets.
- Mutual funds pay no taxes on the income they receive, or on the capital gains they realise. This is logical, since the LIABILITY to tax falls upon those who own the mutual fund shares. There is a caveat, which is that in order to qualify for tax-exempt status, funds must distribute most of the income they get (90% in the United States and 100% of income after costs in the UK, for example). They must also, incidentally, hold a diversified portfolio of assets. In the United States no more than 25% of a fund's assets can be in a single investment and for half a fund's portfolio no more than 5% of assets can be in the securities of a single issuer.

" *The key to making money in stocks is not to get scared of them ... Every year finds a spate of books on how to pick stocks or find the winning mutual fund. But all this information is useless without the will power.*
Peter Lynch, *Beating the Street*

NASDAQ

Short for National Association of Securities Dealers Automated Quotation System. Measured by the volume and value of shares traded, NASDAQ is the world's biggest stock exchange. For example, in June 2008 the average daily volume of shares traded was 2.3 billion with a value of $63.6 billion. However, measured by the market value of the EQUITY of all companies listed on the market, NASDAQ lies third globally, behind the NEW YORK STOCK EXCHANGE and the TOKYO STOCK EXCHANGE. At the end of June 2008, 3,243 securities were listed on NASDAQ.

The market was introduced in 1971 to replace a telephone-based market between members of the NASD, a self-regulated body of dealers and MARKETMAKERS, and it is still sometimes referred to as America's OVER-THE-COUNTER stockmarket, which is true to the extent that NASDAQ has no trading floor. As at June 2008, trading was done by 169 marketmakers, who made markets via a screen-based system of competing quotes. All listed shares must have a least two marketmakers, but although the average number of marketmakers per security is 17, NASDAQ has been criticised for the lack of competition between marketmakers in the prices that they offer, particularly for SMALL CAP STOCKS.

NASDAQ is owned by NASDAQ OMX, whose shares are listed on the NASDAQ exchange and which was formed in May 2007 following NASDAQ's $3.7 billion acquisition of OMX, which operates stock exchanges in Stockholm, Copenhagen, Riga, Helsinki, Tallinn, Vilnius, Reykjavik and Oslo, of which it owns just 10%. In the United States, NASDAQ OMX has also taken over the Philadelphia and Boston stock exchanges.

NASDAQ Europe

A screen-based, quote-driven market, formerly known as EASDAQ (European Association of Securities Dealers Automated Quotation, which was set up in 1996 and struggled for seven years before being closed down in 2003 by NASDAQ, which had owned it since 2001.

Net present value

A net present value (NPV) calculation answers the question: what will be the profit or loss measured in today's money values of an investment opportunity for a given DISCOUNT RATE? If the answer is positive, the present value of all the future cash inflows will be more than all the outflows. In other words, the investment will be profitable.

For example, assume a company is considering a capital project which would entail the following, net of tax cash flows:

Year	*Cash flow ($m)*
0	–20
1	–2
2	2
3	6
4	10
5	15

The project's viability will depend on the discount rate that the company chooses to express the net cash flows in today's values. If it were 8%, the project would generate a $2.2m profit, but if it were 12%, it would be a $1.1m loss. As such, an NPV calculation is similar to an INTERNAL RATE OF RETURN calculation. The latter simply finds the discount rate which would reduce the cash flows to zero. In this example it is 10.6%.

Net worth

The value of a company to its ordinary shareholders as recorded in its BALANCE SHEET. The residual amount left over from a schedule of the company's ASSETS after deducting all the claims on the business which rank ahead of those of the ordinary shareholders. Also known as EQUITY, net assets, or net book value.

Neuer Markt

A stock exchange launched in March 1997 by the DEUTSCHE BÖRSE as part of the FRANKFURT STOCK EXCHANGE for trading shares in technology companies. The Neuer Markt had a successful start and by early 2000 over 200 companies, of which more than 30 were non-German, had an exchange listing. These had a market value of over $85 billion. However, the fall in technology shares meant that the market was closed in June 2003.

New York Stock Exchange

By far the world's biggest stockmarket measured by the market value of the securities listed on the exchange. At the end of 2008, the domestic securities listed on the exchange had a market value of $9.2 trillion. The New York Stock Exchange (NYSE) is owned by NYSE EURONEXT, which was formed in 2007 following the merger of the NYSE and EURONEXT. Its shares are listed on the NYSE. However, it was only in 2005 that the organisation became a for-profit corporation. Until then it was a non-profit corporation, which was owned by its 1,300 members. It traces its history back to 1792 and the so-called Buttonwood Agreement when 24 brokers and merchants formalised arrangements about trading stocks in a deal that was signed under a buttonwood tree outside 68 Wall Street in south Manhattan.

Trading on the exchange, in theory anyway, works through a system of brokers and specialists. The former are the link between the investing public and the market. The latter have a dual role: matching buying and selling orders through an auction system when prevailing prices allow and buying and selling stocks for their own account when this is not possible. Increasingly, however, trading is done by matching buy and sell orders electronically and bypasses the specialists altogether. In the first three months after this system was introduced in 2007, over 80% of trades were executed electronically.

Nikkei 225

Also known as the Nikkei Stock Average, this stockmarket index remains the best-known measure of share values on the TOKYO STOCK EXCHANGE despite its limitations. The Nikkei 225, which was first published in 1950, is composed of 225 shares from the first section (that is, bigger stocks) of the Tokyo exchange. Like the DOW JONES INDUSTRIAL AVERAGE, it is calculated as the unweighted average of the prices of its 225 components with an adjustment made to the denominator to take account of stock splits. In other words, a ¥50 change in the price of the stock will have the same effect on the index's value as a ¥50 price change in any other stock. No allowance is made for the market value of each component.

“ *As a student of human nature, I always have felt that a good speculator should be able to tell what a man will do with his money before he does it.*

Bernard Baruch

Noise trader

A catch-all term used to describe a stockmarket trader who buys and sells securities for all the wrong reasons. Such traders are thus caught up in the noise of the market, seduced into dealing by the gossip and phoney analysis that does the rounds in any big market. Paradoxically, however, they help to make the market efficient by their trading. If they were not around there would be far fewer trades and therefore it would be more difficult to maintain market efficiency (see EFFICIENT MARKET HYPOTHESIS).

NPV

See NET PRESENT VALUE.

NYSE

See NEW YORK STOCK EXCHANGE.

NYSE Composite Index

An index of the stockmarket values of 2,000-plus companies listed on the NEW YORK STOCK EXCHANGE. It began in 1966 with a base level of 50 as at December 31st 1965, but an older index was subsequently incorporated into it giving a continuous price history stretching back to 1939. In January 2003 the index value was rebased to 5,000 since when it peaked at 10,312 in October 2007. It is calculated as a weighted average of the market value of the free float of its constituents. Its value is continuously updated and, therefore, it is suitable for FUTURES contracts to be written against.

NYSE Euronext

The holding company created in 2007 from the merger of the NYSE, which owned the NEW YORK STOCK EXCHANGE, and EURONEXT. The group operates six equities exchanges - two in New York and one each in Paris, Amsterdam, Brussels and Lisbon - and six derivatives exchanges, which include the LONDON INTERNATIONAL FINANCIAL FUTURES AND OPTIONS EXCHANGE.

Odd-lot theory

The stockmarket application of the notion that if you do the opposite of what the dumbest person in town is doing, it is likely to be right. So when amateur investors who deal in odd lots (extremely small amounts of STOCK) buy, it is time to sell, and vice versa. The theory even devises its own index by expressing the ratio of odd-lot sales to odd-lot purchases. Research has shown that odd lotters are not quite as dumb as they are made out to be. Besides, the success of the MUTUAL FUND has undermined the theory because many small-time investors now make their stockmarket investments indirectly via this vehicle.

OEICS

See OPEN-ENDED INVESTMENT COMPANY.

OFEX

See PLUS MARKETS.

Offer price

The price at which dealers will sell securities in the market. It is the higher of the two prices that they will quote for any security in which they make a market. (See also BID PRICE and SPREAD.)

On-the-run bond

A term used to describe the bonds and notes most recently issued by the US Treasury. It is a benchmark security which is heavily traded and thus moves at finer rates than other Treasury securities.

Open-end fund

See MUTUAL FUND.

Open-ended investment company

A type of investment fund which is a cross between a CLOSED-END FUND and a MUTUAL FUND. It has a corporate structure, yet its share capital is variable, rising and falling as investors in aggregate are net buyers or sellers of its shares. Open-ended investment companies (OEICS, pronounced "oiks") are usually arranged as an umbrella fund with a series of subfunds that specialise in particular types of investments. This structure offers savers cheap switching among subfunds with none of the confusion caused by the bid and offer prices at which mutual fund shares are bought and sold.

Open interest

Within a FUTURES market, the open interest is the number of outstanding contracts. But note that for every contract there is both a buyer and a seller. Therefore the open interest changes only when new LONG and SHORT traders are coming into the market, rather than if existing traders are simply covering their positions. Thus open interest can be an indicator of market sentiment; for example, a simultaneous increase in both the SPOT PRICE of an asset and the number of open positions in it in the futures market would imply strong underlying demand.

Open offer

A cheaper way for a company whose shares are already listed on a recognised stock exchange to raise additional capital than through a RIGHTS ISSUE. This is because an open offer does not give existing shareholders PRE-EMPTION RIGHTS over the shares to be issued, thus saving administration costs and underwriting fees. The term "open offer" is a misnomer because the new shares are generally placed with institutional investors by the company's advisers. Existing shareholders usually have the right to claw back new shares at a rate determined by their existing holding. However, because an open offer will not depend on the approval of existing shareholders in a ballot, this right has no market value. In the UK, companies are generally restricted to increasing their issued share capital by no more than 15% a year through open offers and this power is subject to approval by shareholders annually.

Open outcry

The way in which trading is carried out on some FUTURES and OPTIONS exchanges. It is a continuous auction process, which takes place on the floor of the exchange among dealers, to buy and sell contracts. Although it looks chaotic, unruly even, it is an efficient way of trading, especially in less liquid contracts. It depends on dealers using a combination of shouting and hand signals to show whether they are buying or selling, what their price is and how many contracts they are dealing in.

Option

The best-known of all types of DERIVATIVES, an option gives the holder the right, but not the obligation, to buy or sell a specific amount of an ASSET, probably ORDINARY SHARES, at a specified price within a specific period. Correspondingly, a person who underwrites an options contract accepts the obligation to deliver or buy shares according to the terms of the contract. In return, the buyer of the contract pays that person a fee upfront.

Options are not new. They were introduced in London as far back as the early 18th century and, indeed, they were banned from the LONDON STOCK EXCHANGE from 1734 to 1860. However, their formal trading on exchanges has been confined to the last 30 years or so when they were introduced first on the CHICAGO BOARD OF TRADE in 1973 and then on the London exchange in 1978. In London they are known as traded options to distinguish them from conventional options, which are basically OVER-THE-COUNTER contracts. A further confusion is that there are American-style and European-style options. However, most trading is in the American-style instrument, even in Europe. The difference is that the holder of an American-style option can exercise the right to buy or sell the underlying STOCK at any time before the contract expires; with a European-style option the right to exercise comes only when the contract expires.

Options are either CALL OPTIONS or PUT OPTIONS. Calls give the holder the right to buy shares at a specific price; puts give the right to sell shares. Contracts are standardised so that in the UK, where share prices are generally smaller, one contract gives rights over 1,000 shares and in the United States one contract generally gives rights over 100 shares. In both the UK and the United States, option contracts have the same pattern of expiry cycles. So, for example, the cycle beginning in January will have contracts which expire in April, July and October. The other cycles are: February, May, August, November; and March, June, September, December. All stocks which have traded options will be allocated to one of these cycles. This means that the maximum term of any option contract is nine months. However, in the United States there are shorter, infill cycles so that leading stocks will have options contracts ending almost every month of the year.

Options are banded together in "series", which are defined by their expiry date and their EXERCISE PRICE. For example, a company's January 110 calls would be one series and its April 110 calls would be another. Initially, 12 series would be introduced for each underlying security, six for the calls and six for the puts. Within each group of six, three series would be for contracts above the prevailing price of the underlying security (one for each expiry date) and three for contracts below it. Then further series would be introduced as the price of the stock shifts, which is why the options pages of the financial press can quote so many series of options in a stock at any one time.

> *Why do people forever try to link the economy with the stockmarket. Economics have nothing to do with timing – and timing is everything.*
> Joe Granville

Options premium

The amount of cash that the buyer of an OPTIONS contract pays and a seller (or WRITER) receives. In the market premiums are quoted on a per-share basis, but contracts are actually sold for lots of 1,000 shares (100 in the United States). So if a premium is quoted at 30p, a buyer pays £300 plus dealing costs. The premium itself can be analysed into two components: its INTRINSIC VALUE and its TIME VALUE (or speculative value).

Ordinary share

The security that companies issue in return for high-risk capital. Such capital is high-risk because it ranks behind other forms of capital in its claims on the income and ASSETS of the corporation. The RISK, however, is limited to the value of the ordinary shares; that is, if the business fails, creditors and owners of other types of capital can make no claim on the shareholders beyond the funds they already have in the business. The corollary to risk is that ordinary shares carry unlimited potential for gains because other forms of capital have only fixed claims on the business. Shareholders also have ownership rights. They can vote directors in and out of office, approve their own DIVIDENDS, change the nature of the company, even liquidate it if they wish. Most of the time these rights are more theoretical than real, but if they are sufficiently motivated, shareholders can exercise them.

OTC

See OVER-THE-COUNTER.

Out of the money

In options, a CALL OPTION is out of the money when the market price of the shares it can buy is lower than the price at which the options contract can be exercised. For example, if a company's shares trade at 100p, options to buy the shares at 110p and 120p would be out of the money, although an option to buy at 90p would be IN THE MONEY. For a PUT OPTION, which is the right to sell shares at a specific price, the opposite is the case. A put option is out of the money when the market price is higher than the price at which the option can be exercised.

Over-the-counter

A generic term used to describe trading in securities by any means other than via a recognised stock exchange. Essentially an over-the-counter (OTC) trade is a bilateral contract where two parties agree the details of a transaction involving securities or DERIVATIVES. OTC trading takes in almost all trading done in the EUROBOND market and in ASSET-backed securities in general. As such, volumes of securities traded far outstrip the volumes done on any single stock exchange.

Pac-man defence

A tactic used by a company's management when facing a hostile takeover bid from another company. It comprises countering with a takeover bid for the original aggressor. The tactic is named after a video game of the 1980s in which all characters have to swallow their opponent or be consumed themselves.

Pari passu

Literally, with equal ranking. A phrase used in corporate documents to indicate that new shares issued by a company carry the same rights over income and assets as existing shares.

Paris Bourse

The Paris stock exchange, which drove the creation of EURONEXT in 2000 through the merger of the Paris, Brussels and Amsterdam stock exchanges. Paris is the most important of the three. At the end of November 2008 the market value of French EQUITIES was €1,081 billion, which accounts for about half the market value of Euronext equities. The Paris Bourse is now an independently operating part of Euronext, offering trading in all the major listed equities on the three exchanges and trading medium-sized and small company shares through its Alternext market, a lightly regulated exchange that was opened in 2005. Trading is done by an electronic order-driven system, which has been upgraded since its introduction in 1986 to form the trading platform for all Euronext equities exchanges. Paris also has a *marché libre*, which matches buy and sell orders for unlisted shares, but trades are not covered by the market's counterparty guarantee.

Payback period

The length of time that it takes for an investment to generate sufficient cumulative CASH FLOW to pay back its cost. It is a simple measure, mostly used by companies to evaluate capital spending projects. Adjusting the cash flow by applying a DISCOUNT RATE to account for RISK can make it more useful.

PEP

See next entry.

P/E ratio

See PRICE/EARNINGS RATIO.

Personal equity plan

A tax-break scheme introduced in 1987 in the UK to encourage "popular capitalism". Personal equity plans (PEPS) sheltered shareholdings from capital gains and income taxes. In return for the tax breaks, PEP schemes required that funds were invested mainly in EU-domiciled companies and there were strict limits on the amount that could be invested in each tax year. PEPS were abolished at the end of the 1998/99 tax year.

PLUS Markets

London's third EQUITY market (in addition to the LONDON STOCK EXCHANGE'S full list and the ALTERNATIVE INVESTMENT MARKET), which began trading in late 2006 as a replacement for OFEX. PLUS Markets is both an electronic trading platform (PLUS-listed), which offers trading in all London's listed shares and others besides, and a market in quoted companies' shares (PLUS-quoted) in its own right. As at mid-2008, shares in 221 companies were quoted on PLUS-quoted with a market value of £2.3 billion.

Point and figure chart

An unusual way of plotting the price changes of an investment because the horizontal axis plots time, but not in specific regular intervals. The aim is to find areas where lots of price changes are compressed into a short period as this is supposed to presage a price break-out of the investment concerned. Only significant

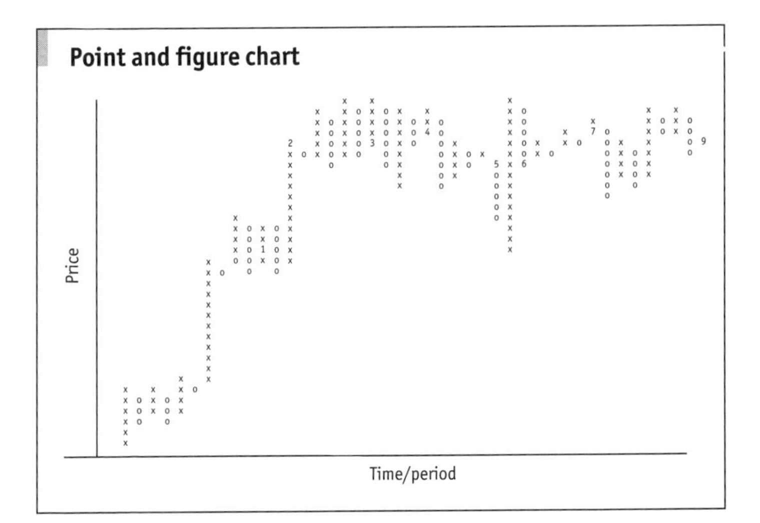

Point and figure chart

changes are plotted at all; say, when the price of the investment moves by 10p. As long as the changes are in the same direction they are stacked vertically, usually using X for an upward move and O for a fall. When the direction of movement switches, as well as changing the sign (from X to O or vice versa) the plots are shifted one column to the right. Thus when the price oscillates up and down the chart is stretched out horizontally, indicating that all-important break-out.

Poison pill

A device, somewhat euphemistically called a shareholders' rights plan, which aims to protect a company from a hostile takeover bid. It is a legal contract giving shareholders of a target company rights which, if exercised, would make the takeover of the company prohibitively expensive. The most familiar variant of the plan gives shareholders in the target company the right to buy substantial numbers of new shares at a big discount to the market price in the event of a hostile bid. Since they were introduced in 1982 poison pills have swept corporate America, and in the late 1990s more than two-thirds of companies in the S&P 500 INDEX had adopted them. However, they are criticised for depressing the share price of companies and keeping inefficient managements in office. As a consequence, increasingly the trend is for shareholders to vote against their authorisation.

Pooling of interests

A method of accounting for the merger of two companies which has the prime advantages that the transaction creates no accounting GOODWILL (which would have to be amortised against profits) and that the distributable reserves of both companies are available for future distribution to stockholders. However, pooling of interests was just one of two distinct methods used to account for acquisitions (the other being purchase accounting, where one company is always deemed to have taken over the other), and in the interests of consistency pooling of interests has been scrapped under the accounting rules of both the United States and the European Union.

Portfolio theory

Investors intuitively know that there is a trade-off between RISK and return (that is, the greater the rewards they seek the bigger the risks they have to take and vice versa). It is equally intuitive that diversifying investments reduces risk because within a portfolio the value of some holdings will go up as that of others goes down. The aim of portfolio theory is to provide a mathematical framework to explain how and why this happens and from there to make predictions for expected returns for portfolios in the real world.

The theory was originally formalised by Harry Markovitz in the early 1950s. He began by defining risk as the variability of returns from an average and proved that risk within a portfolio was not simply the weighted average risk of the portfolio's components, but that it could be reduced to less than the weighted average by means of diversification. Simultaneously, however, the returns on the portfolio would always be the weighted average of the components' returns. The implications of this were substantial: it is not only diversification that matters, but also how you diversify. From this came the idea of the EFFICIENT PORTFOLIO, one that produces the greatest returns for a specific level of risk or carries the least risk for a given return. So there must be an efficient portfolio for every increment of risk or return, giving rise to the concept of the EFFICIENT FRONTIER, the line on a chart which joins up all the efficient portfolios across the risk or return spectrum.

Simplifying Markovitz's model was the next stage in the development. He arrived at a portfolio's risk or return trade-off by calculating how every pair of investments in a portfolio moved in relation to each other. This required a formidable amount of work. It was also unnecessary because it was increasingly clear that STOCKS, to which the theory was largely applied anyway, moved up or down in relation to the whole market as much as in relation to each other. So it was sensible to use the relation between a stockmarket index and each stock as the basis for calculating risk. This produced the SINGLE INDEX MODEL as a way of generating efficient portfolios, a method which involved much less work and produced portfolios similar to the full Markovitz workings.

Nowadays the single index model is used to work out efficient portfolios with many components. But where few components are involved, for example in allocating funds across the world's major stockmarkets, the Markovitz model remains the preferred choice because it examines the relationship between each pair of investments in the portfolio. (See also CAPITAL ASSET PRICING MODEL and CAPITAL MARKET THEORY.)

Pre-emption rights

The rights of shareholders to maintain their proportionate ownership of a company. Thus when a company has a RIGHTS ISSUE, shareholders must be offered their pro-rata entitlement to new shares, which, consequently, have a market value that can be realised. However, in both the United States and the UK, especially the former, pre-emption rights are being eroded. In the United States the SECURITIES AND EXCHANGE COMMISSION, which regulates all STOCK issues, has not insisted that new stock be offered to existing stockholders when a corporation can raise new capital more cheaply by another means. That is frequently the case because the time and work involved in rights issues means that they are an expensive way of raising capital.

Preference share

Technically part of the EQUITY capital of a company, thus carrying limited ownership rights, a preference share is better analysed as a hybrid form of debt. Its claims on a company are for a fixed DIVIDEND every year which, if not paid, usually accrues until it can be, and for repayment of its par value in the event of a winding up. Preference shareholders rank behind holders of debt in their claims, but ahead of the holders of ORDINARY SHARES. Generally, preference shares carry no voting rights, but this can change in some circumstances, usually if their dividends are in arrears. Often they come with rights to convert into ordinary shares, in which case they usually have a fixed term before being repaid. Such shares can be valued as convertibles. Still, the majority of preference shares in issue are irredeemable and, therefore, given the fixed nature of their income, can be valued by grossing up the annual income by the required rate of return.

Preferred stock

See PREFERENCE SHARE.

Premium

This has a variety of meanings within the world of investment, but the two most important are as follows:

- It is what the buyer of an options contract pays to acquire the contract.
- It means that one figure is in excess of another. For example, a CLOSED-END FUND's ordinary shares would be at a premium to the fund's net ASSETS per share if they traded in the market for more than the BALANCE SHEET value of the attributable assets per share.

Price/earnings ratio

A ubiquitous investment tool for analysing the cheapness or dearness of ORDINARY SHARES. The success of price/earnings ratios (P/E ratios) derives from two things: their utter simplicity – the ratio is just the price of a share divided by a measure of its attributable EARNINGS; and the intuitive ease with which they can be handled – a high P/E ratio implies that the market expects faster-than-average future growth from a share, and a low P/E ratio implies the opposite. However, this means that every tip sheet and investment analyst who can think of nothing better uses a low P/E ratio as a reason to recommend buying a share.

In practice, investment analysts use P/E ratios to make comparisons between shares and the whole market or, more likely, between a share and its peer group. Thus utilities, for example, have traditionally traded on a ratio below the market average. The test of whether the shares of a utilities group are cheap, therefore, is not how they are rated in relation to the market (they will almost certainly be lower), but whether they will have a low P/E ratio relative to their sector. To determine this, analysts must look not at current earnings but at future earnings. The trouble is they rarely look far enough because the P/E ratio, like its close cousin the DIVIDEND DISCOUNT MODEL, is basically a discounting mechanism. Thus it reflects the present value that the market gives to all the future earnings and DIVIDENDS that a company will generate.

To explain, assume that a company is expected to pay a dividend of 10.5p per share for a full year; that its dividends are expected to grow constantly at 5% a year; and that an investor requires a 12% annual return from holding the shares. The constant growth dividend discount model would value such shares at 150p each by dividing the 10.5p dividend by the difference between the 12% required rate and the 5% expected growth rate. The sum is $10.5 \div (0.12 - 0.05)$.

This basic model can be adapted to calculate the appropriate P/E ratio by applying the company's expected earnings to the equation. Assume earnings are forecast to be 20p. Then the P/E ratio sum becomes (10.5 ÷ 20) ÷ (0.12 – 0.05). (See Appendix 5 for the algebraic formula.) This works out at 7.5 times earnings, which squares with the dividend discount model's valuation of 150p since 7.5 times 20p equals 150p.

These workings provide a basic model, but one which is especially sensitive to changes in the bottom-line variables, which themselves are always arrived at fairly subjectively. If the gap between the required rate and the expected dividend growth rate narrows, the P/E ratio – and implicitly the share price – rises enormously and vice versa.

So P/E ratios have their uses, even if they are a limited tool. Nevertheless, not enough thought is given to the idea that the P/E ratio simply reflects the correct value of a share instead of the assumed notion that the search for the correct P/E ratio drives the share price.

> “ *Of the maxims of orthodox finance, none, surely, is more anti-social than the fetish of liquidity, the doctrine that it is a positive virtue on the part of investment institutions to concentrate their resources upon the holding of "liquid" securities.*
>
> John Maynard Keynes, *The General Theory of Employment, Interest and Money* (1936)

Price-to-book ratio

The ratio between the market price of an ORDINARY SHARE and the BOOK VALUE per share. Thus it is a measure of the value that the market awards to the shareholders' funds employed in a business. The higher the ratio then implicitly the more highly the market rates the company and the better are its prospects. This may be because investors believe that the true value of its ASSETS is much higher than shown in its books, or that the likely future growth in EARNINGS will be sufficient to merit a high price-to-book ratio.

Alternatively, a low ratio may be particularly interesting to a follower of VALUE INVESTING because, in an extreme case where the stock price is below book value, investors are getting more than a pound of book value for every pound of stock they buy. The test will be whether the market knows something that individual investors do not when it values the stock so low.

The ratio is also applied across the whole stockmarket as an indicator of cheapness or expensiveness. For example, the price-to-book ratio for the S&P 500 INDEX has historically been mostly in the range of two to four times. However, by early 2000 it had risen to over six times at which point the most severe BEAR market for 25 years set in.

Private equity

A branch of ASSET management in which funds own substantial stakes in the EQUITY of companies – often the whole company – whose shares are not traded on recognised stock exchanges.

From its origins shortly after the second world war, private equity made little impact until the 1980s, when it helped the development of technology companies such as Microsoft, Apple and Cisco. Since then its growth has magnified movements in the global economy, faltering in the early 1990s and the early 2000s but by and large growing rapidly, so that in 2005 globally private equity funds raised $232 billion and invested $135 billion.

In the past its major source of funds was wealthy individuals but, as the industry's size and profile expanded, it has attracted increasing amounts of funds from conventional institutional investors, such as pension funds and insurance companies.

The chief selling point of private equity is that it can generate higher returns than those available from investment in publicly traded equity. Private equity fund managers claim to be able to do this because companies owned by their funds can take a longer-term perspective than companies whose shares are subject to the listing requirements of stock exchanges and because of their superior management skills. In the case of more mature businesses, this is often achieved by loading them up with debt (whose interest costs attract a tax credit), cutting costs to the bone and seeking an exit in the medium term, say after 3–5 years.

On average, however, it is doubtful that private equity funds generate net returns for their outside investors that are superior to those available from publicly quoted equity investments. This is partly because of the high fees that most managers charge. That said, the difference between the best- and worst-performing funds is dramatic and – contrary to what PORTFOLIO THEORY indicates – there may be a core of private equity fund managers that can consistently produce top-of-the-range performance.

See also VENTURE CAPITAL.

Probability theory

The application of mathematics to games of chance, of which investment can be considered one. Probability theory was developed in the 17th century, in particular by Blaise Pascal and Pierre de Fermat, and is essentially the mathematical explanation of the likelihood of an event occurring.

Say that in order to make an accurate forecast of a company's profits an investment analyst must accurately forecast eight components of financial performance (change in revenues, change in costs, and so on). Even if the chance of forecasting each component accurately is as high as one in two (that is, a probability of 0.5, the same odds as correctly calling the toss of a coin), the chance of accurately forecasting all eight components (and therefore the company's profits) is just one in 256 (or 2 raised to the power of 8). Put another way, the analyst's task of forecasting eight components can produce 256 outcomes, only one of which is wholly accurate.

The trouble is that when company bosses make their deals, when analysts make their forecasts and when investors buy their shares, they generally forget probability theory and overestimate their chances of success.

> *When it is not in our power to determine what is true, we ought to act in accordance with what is most probable.*
> René Descartes

Profit margin

A key measure of a company's financial performance that essentially expresses profit per unit of sales. In other words, profit margin equals profits as a percentage of sales, or revenues, for an accounting period. Analysts can finesse which measure of profit they use as the numerator. Most often they take operating profits before interest and taxes, which excludes any one-off items such as profits on disposals or reorganisation costs.

There is no absolute scale of good or bad profit margin. However, the more capital that a company employs to generate a given amount of revenue, the higher its profit margin must be to justify the use of the capital. For example, take two companies, both of which produce $100m of revenue in the same financial year. If one employs capital of just $25m, it will generate a 20% RETURN ON CAPITAL if its profit margin is 5% – the sum is (100 ÷ 25) × 5. However, if the other employs $50m of capital, its profit margin must be 10% to make the same return on capital. Contrast with MARGIN.

Program trading

Since the stockmarket crash of October 1987, program trading has been singled out as a cause of much of the instability on the world's major stockmarkets, especially Wall Street. The claim is difficult to prove, although clearly one type of program trading, INDEX ARBITRAGE, can cause sudden sharp movements in STOCK prices when positions are unwound. Program trading, however, is a more generic term for a variety of stockmarket strategies which embrace the aim of automatically rebalancing the weightings of assets in an investment portfolio through the use of OPTIONS, FUTURES and the underlying securities. As such, it is not in itself inherently destabilising. However, it is monitored closely and often accounts for more than 20% of equities trading done on the NEW YORK STOCK EXCHANGE each week, occasionally exceeding 30%.

Put hedge

A popular strategy in OPTIONS trading to insure a shareholding or an entire share portfolio against possible future losses while retaining the right to gain from possible future price rises. Basically, an investor buys PUT OPTIONS whose value will rise in the event of a fall in the price of the underlying shares, thus cancelling out some or all of the losses depending on how far the holding is fully hedged. If the share price does not actually fall, the put option will expire worthless, but this can be seen as the cost of an insurance policy which was never used.

Put option

Buying put options fulfils the archetypal bearish strategy because puts give the owner of a put contract the right, but not the obligation, to sell a STOCK at a specific price within a specified period. So if someone thinks that the price of an ORDINARY SHARE will fall in the coming months, the right to sell the stock above its market price will have value and will become more valuable the further the stock's market price falls. Thus a put option is the mirror image of a CALL OPTION, although it is less intuitively easy to understand.

Take a simple example. Assume that the price of a share in a company stands in the market at 380p and a put option is available for 10p, giving the right to sell the share at 370p. A BEAR who buys this put must believe that the price of the share will fall below 360p (the 370p at which he has the right to sell minus the 10p cost of acquiring that right) before the option expires. If it does not, the bear will lose money, but his maximum losses will always be pegged at 10p no matter how high the share price rises. However, if the price does fall, the value of the put will rise as the share price falls.

Thus puts, as well as providing an insurance policy for someone who holds the underlying shares, also provide an attractive speculation through the LEVERAGE that they offer. In the admittedly oversimplified example, if the price of the share falls to 340p, the speculator using puts would have made 20p for an outlay of 10p, a profit of 100%. Alternatively, he could have sold the shares SHORT at 380p and bought them back at 340p, but this would have realised only 40p profit, or 12%.

If you know why you bought a stock in the first place, you'll automatically have a better idea of when to say goodbye to it.
Peter Lynch, American investor

Qualitative analysis

That part of investment analysis, almost always of ORDINARY SHARES, which requires some element of subjectivity. The qualitative assessment of a corporation would include taking a view on the prospects for the industry in which it operates, the strength of its competition and the ability of its management.

Quantitative analysis

Crunching numbers in order to determine whether a proposed investment passes muster, rather than using qualitative judgments. In analysing a single company, quantitative analysis would entail calculating various ratios from the INCOME STATEMENT, BALANCE SHEET and CASH FLOW statements. To find a portfolio of shares, the exercise would involve selecting those securities which pass various quantitative tests; a simple one might be sufficient DIVIDEND YIELD, high RETURN ON CAPITAL, low PRICE/EARNINGS RATIO. The identity of the investments is much less important than their ability to pass statistical tests. In practice, however, the distinction between qualitative and quantitative elements becomes blurred, although there is a case for saying that the qualitative aspects of an investment are revealed in the quantitative findings.

R&D

See RESEARCH AND DEVELOPMENT.

R-squared

A statistic that quantifies the proportion of VARIANCE in a STOCK's return that can be explained by the variance in the return from the market of which the stock is a part. In CAPITAL MARKET THEORY, REGRESSION ANALYSIS is widely used to predict stock returns. However, such analysis can only predict returns on average and in the real world there is a wide dispersion around the average. So R^2 measures the degree of fit between the market's returns and the stock returns. The higher the R^2, the more of the stock's return is predicted by the market's return.

Random walk

A branch of the EFFICIENT MARKET HYPOTHESIS that has probably generated more hot air than any other part of PORTFOLIO THEORY. To say that STOCK prices move along a random walk is explicitly to insult those who believe in the merits of TECHNICAL ANALYSIS and implicitly to insult adherents of FUNDAMENTAL ANALYSIS. Random walk says that the day-to-day changes in the market price of a stock are random. Therefore, tomorrow's closing price, or any future price, cannot be predicted on the basis of past closing prices. When price-sensitive information arrives the stock price will rightly change, but the arrival of that news is entirely random. Therefore the stock's price follows a random walk around the stock's INTRINSIC VALUE.

The major consequence of random walk is that past patterns of stock price changes become irrelevant in trying to predict future prices. In other words, it is not possible to make excess returns from analysing price patterns; therefore technical analysis is not worth the effort. Furthermore, if price changes are random it becomes debatable whether fundamental analysis is worthwhile, since acting upon price-sensitive announcements by corporations would not generate excess returns in the long run (the successes and failures would even themselves out).

In spite of all this, it remains – and is likely to remain – unproven whether stock prices do follow a random walk. The only certainty is that the debate will continue.

Real

A little word that often crops up in investment jargon. Essentially it means "after taking account of inflation". So the real return on a stockmarket would be the nominal percentage change in its index over a specified period adjusted for the rate of inflation over the same period. However, some confusion arises in the use of real returns. If a company's shares paid a DIVIDEND that generated a YIELD of 5% in a year and the inflation rate was 3%, it would be wrong to say the real yield on the shares was 2%. All that has actually happened is that the real value of the dividend has been eroded by 3%. So, to be precise, and assuming that the dividend was paid at the end of the period, the yield would be 4.85% after accounting for inflation.

Real estate investment trust

Abbreviated to REIT (pronounced "reet"), these are corporations that do for investing in real estate (property) what CLOSED-END FUNDS do for investing in equities. In other words, they are so-called "pass-through" entities, which means that they have freedom from corporation tax so long as they distribute – that is, pass through – almost all of their income. In both the United States and the UK the proportion of income that has to be distributed is at least 90% to pick up this benefit. The other major stipulation is that a REIT must invest almost all of its capital in property and must derive almost all of its income – 95% in the United States – from that source. However, it can come from DIVIDENDS from other property companies, interest from MORTGAGES as well as rents from properties owned. In the UK, a company's shares must be listed on a recognised stock exchange for it to have REIT status. But in the United States a REIT's shares do not have to be publicly traded, although they do have to be owned by at least 100 investors for the company to keep its tax benefits.

Redemption yield

See YIELD TO MATURITY.

Registered security

A security that is recorded in the name of the owner on a register kept by the issuer or the issuer's agent. DIVIDENDS or interest are automatically paid to the owner and transfer of ownership can take place only with the owner's consent. Most shares are registered, as are government-issued BONDS.

Regression analysis

A major tool of economics which finds uses in investment analysis. Regression analysis is about using statistical techniques to test the relationship between two or more variables in a mathematical model and to discover, therefore, whether it is reasonable to infer that past relationships will hold good in the future. Consequently, it is rigorously applied to the major models of investment analysis: the BLACK-SCHOLES OPTION PRICING MODEL, the CAPITAL ASSET PRICING MODEL and the main branches of PORTFOLIO THEORY.

Reinvestment rate

A crucial element in investment calculations that show a staggeringly big sum being generated from a comparatively small starting amount is the reinvestment rate chosen. This is the rate of return applied to the income that is produced by the capital. Clearly, the higher the reinvestment rate and the further the investment horizon, the bigger is the final sum.

For example, imagine that $1,000 is tied up for 20 years and it generates $100 of income every year, therefore $2,000 over the whole investment period. If that income is reinvested to obtain a return of 15% per year over the period, the total of income plus interest on the income will be $8,900; that is, $6,900 will have come from reinvesting and just $2,000 from the original income. However, if the reinvestment rate was only 5%, the total sum would be $3,154, with just $1,154 coming from reinvested income. This is quite a contrast.

By using as the rate for reinvesting income the rate at which an investment fund's capital grows, massive future sums can be generated from modest starting amounts. This is a familiar marketing trick used for MUTUAL FUNDS. The question is whether they are available in the real world. Regular savings plans for managed funds mean that returns at least approaching the reinvestment rate are accessible, but for those investing directly in shares, attaining a reinvestment rate equal to the capital growth achieved might be another matter.

REIT

See REAL ESTATE INVESTMENT FUND.

Repo

A sale-and-repurchase agreement between two parties, usually associated with using marketable government debt as security for the transaction. In the United States, for example, there is a massive repo market in US Treasury notes and BONDS and in the UK a Bank of England-approved repo market was introduced in 1996. The seller of the STOCK effectively raises a loan which will be repaid with interest by repurchasing the stock at a predetermined price. The buyer has title to the stock, but contracts to deliver equivalent securities at the agreed date.

For investors a liquid repo market means they can cheaply finance positions in the underlying market for government stock. For example, an investor who buys $10m of ten-year Treasury notes can immediately sell the notes in the repo market to finance his purchase. Rates of interest are keen because the collateral is risk-free government debt. The person buying in the stock is termed "reversing in" to the security. If he instigated the transaction to cover a SHORT position in the cash market, technically the deal is not a repo but a "reverse".

For governments the attraction of a well-developed repo market, in which their debt effectively takes on the characteristics of cash, is cheaper borrowing costs. Central banks also use repos on their own account to influence interest rates in the wider economy. Either they sell marketable debt for future repurchase to drain funds out of the banking system and push up rates, or they temporarily buy in bonds in order to reduce rates.

 *Business. It's quite simple. It's other people's money.*
Alexander Dumas

Research and development

The costs that companies run up in developing new products and bringing them to the market. For some types of company, notably pharmaceuticals and electronics businesses, these are substantial costs, so how they are treated becomes a material issue. Mostly companies write them off against income as the costs are incurred. However, some treat research and development (R&D) costs as the development of a future income stream and therefore CAPITALISE them as an ASSET in their BALANCE SHEETS.

Residual income

The amount of profit left in a business after it has paid both its explicit cost of debt and its implicit cost of EQUITY for an accounting period. In other words, for a business to be successful it must generate residual income; that is, its after-tax profits must be sufficient to service the debt costs of its lenders and the cost of its equity capital, which is an opportunity cost determined by the return that investors expect from holding a company's shares. Because residual income takes into account both the cost of debt and equity, it is the only measure that truly assesses corporate profitability, say its supporters. Indeed, focusing on residual income has become fashionable among company chiefs and investment analysts, especially in the United States, and tools to measure it, ironing out various accounting anomalies, are marketed under various guises. However, academic research has shown that the correlation between companies generating large amounts of residual income and superior share-price performance is no stronger than the link between conventional accounting profits and share returns.

Return on capital

Arguably one of the most useful ratios in assessing the performance of a company. It should show the percentage return that a company generates from the capital that it uses. So just as a savings account paying a higher rate of interest is better than one paying a lower rate, then, other things being equal, a company generating a high return on capital is better than one generating a lower return. The trouble is things rarely remain the same, and the challenge with calculating return on capital figures that are comparable both across time and among companies is to use numbers that are consistent and sensible, particularly for the amount of capital employed.

The basic sum, however, is simple; it is a measure of profit expressed as a percentage of the capital employed to generate the profit. Take the following example.

	Year 1	*Year 2*
	$m	*$m*
Shareholders' equity	3,863	4,622
Preference shares	14	16
Long-term debt	1,156	1,512
Short-term debt	711	706
Deferred taxes & allowances	578	529
Capital employed	**6,322**	**7,385**
Average capital employed		6,854
Average equity employed		4,243
Operating profit before interest		1,017
Net profit after taxes		539
Return on capital (%)		14.8
Return on equity (%)		**12.7**

These points are worth noting:

- The capital employed – $6,322m in year 1 and $7,385 in year 2 – is the gross amount of shareholders' EQUITY plus interest-bearing capital; that is, short-term creditors which have no explicit cost are excluded.
- The return on capital is profits before interest and taxes as a percentage of the capital employed.
- The equity employed is just the ordinary shareholders' interest in the business (that is, it excludes the preference capital shown in the table).
- Return on equity is profits after interest, taxes and preference shareholders' DIVIDENDS as a percentage of equity employed.
- Both ratios are based on "average" capital employed; that is, the mid-point between the two years. So in this example, return on capital is calculated as $1,017m as a percentage of $6,854m and return on equity is $539m as a percentage of $4,243m.
- Return on capital could be adjusted so that loan capital gets the same tax treatment as equity; that is, the interest is no longer tax deductible. This helps comparisons between companies with differing levels of debt.
- The amount of capital employed can be calculated from using either side of the BALANCE SHEET.
- Many further adjustments can be made, but the golden rule is to be consistent.

Reverse yield gap

See YIELD GAP.

Rights issue

A means by which a company raises new capital, most often EQUITY but it can be convertible capital. The essential principle behind a rights issue is that existing shareholders in the company have the right to maintain both their proportionate voting power and their proportionate share of the company's profits and ASSETS. Thus the new capital is offered to them first. This brings problems caused by the time and effort involved in notifying all shareholders and giving them sufficient time to decide if they want to take up the issue. As time equals money, rights are criticised as an expensive way for a company to raise new capital. However, when managements do use rights issues (and they remain the major way in which companies in the UK raise new equity) they still do their best to persuade shareholders that they are getting a good deal.

In fact, rights issues neither create nor destroy value for shareholders, whether they accept the issue or not. Take the following simple example. A company offers shareholders one new share at 300p for every three shares they already own (assume that the market price of existing shares is 350p). This means that for every three shares (market value £10.50) that shareholders own, they have the right to add another for £3. They have a choice. Either they can make a pro-rata investment of £3 for each new share, bringing their holding to four shares with a value of £13.50 (£10.50 plus £3); or they can keep their three shares and sell the rights to the fourth in the market. If they opt for the latter course, then, other things being equal, the market value of their three "old" shares will fall to £10.13 (three-quarters of £13.50), leaving them 37p SHORT on the value of their original holding. However, a conventional formula for valuing rights will produce the figure 37p as the value of the right to buy the new share for 300p. Thus the shareholders are back where they started with the option to use their £3 as they please.

The figures do not often work out quite so neatly in real life. This is partly because in the UK, although not in the United States, the sale of rights can create a tax LIABILITY. The details of the calculation also depend on how the market reacts to the news of the company's rights issue.

> *I'm only interested in what we can lose. The downside risk is something I constantly hammer home to my people involved in acquisitions. I say: "Don't worry about how much you can make, how much can you lose?"*
>
> Lord White, co-founder, Hanson

Risk

The flipside of return. If investors want anything more than the RISK-FREE RATE OF RETURN from an investment, they must bear some degree of risk. In other words, risk is the possibility that an investment will not turn out as well as expected. Within PORTFOLIO THEORY it is defined as the variability of returns, using either STANDARD DEVIATION or BETA, both of which are measures of VOLATILITY. Portfolio theory asserts that some risks can be eliminated by holding a diversified bunch of investments (UNSYSTEMATIC RISK), but some cannot be diversified away (SYSTEMATIC RISK) because they are risks that are the concomitant of investing in a particular market.

Risk and reward

The conflict that lies at the heart of investment: if RISK is the possibility that an investment will not deliver the rewards expected, these possible rewards must rise as the likelihood of their eventual delivery recedes. Thus investors can make worthwhile rewards only by taking risks. Logically this must be so. If there were big rewards to be made without taking risks, everyone would chase after them and by the process of ARBITRAGE they would be priced away.

Whether this is so in practice is debatable. The fact that year-in, year-out some professional investors can make excess returns indicates that they have found the ticket to a perpetual free lunch. Alternatively, they may simply be lucky. There are enough professional investors in the world with verifiable investment records for the notion to hold good that the few consistently successful ones are no more than the stockmarket equivalent of the people who always make the right call in a COIN-FLIPPING CONTEST.

“ *It takes patience, discipline and courage to follow the contrarian route to investment success: to buy when others are despondently selling, to sell when others are avidly buying.*

John Templeton, founder, Templeton Growth Fund

Risk arbitrage

A contradiction in terms, but nevertheless a term that has come to have real meaning in the hectic world of corporate raiding. Risk arbitrage aims to make an automatic profit if an event takes place, but if the event does not occur there is no profit, hence the RISK. For example, if a company has made a hostile bid for another, a risk arbitrager (the colloquial term is “arb”) might buy shares in the potential victim on the assumption that the bid has to be raised for it to succeed. Similarly, if the bidder is using its own shares to finance the potential deal, the arb might sell the bidder's shares and buy the victim's with the aim of acquiring cheap shares in the combined corporation. If there are OPTIONS in the shares of either or both corporations, the potential for arbs to demonstrate how smart they are becomes greater still.

Risk-free asset

An investment that carries a RISK-FREE RATE OF RETURN.

Risk-free rate of return

The return on an investment which, for a given period, carries no RISK – the return is effectively guaranteed. This has important implications for PORTFOLIO THEORY. Imagine that a portfolio of assets whose returns are risky (that is, their final outcome is not known) is combined with a risk-free asset. Then, for a specified level of risk, the enlarged portfolio will always produce a superior return to a portfolio comprising only risky assets. This is because the overall return on any portfolio will always be the average of the returns of the investments it contains weighted by their proportions, but the risk will comprise only the weighted average of the risky investments. This has to be so since the risk-free asset, by definition, carries zero risk.

The substitute for the risk-free rate of return is always the return offered on government debt for the time horizon under consideration. So if, for example, an investment analyst is considering the best investments with a five-year horizon, the risk-free rate would be whatever is the YIELD TO MATURITY on five-year Treasury notes. Although the price of these notes would bounce around within the five-year period, the timing and amount of their DIVIDENDS plus their value on redemption would be known with certainty in advance, therefore their risk-free rate of return could be calculated with equal certainty.

Rule of 72

A rule of thumb that says how many years it will take for an investment to double for a given annual COMPOUND RETURN.

The number of years is found by dividing the interest rate into 72. So an investment growing at 10% a year will take 7.2 years to double. Conversely, the equation can be rearranged to discover the rate of interest. If an investment doubles over five years, its compound rate of growth has been $72 \div 5 = 14.4\%$.

Rule of twenty

A useful little investment rule that says that the PRICE/EARNINGS RATIO of a stockmarket plus the inflation rate in the domestic economy should equal 20. So if the P/E ratio on the NEW YORK STOCK EXCHANGE were 16 times, the prevailing inflation rate should be 4% or thereabouts. For both the US and the UK EQUITY markets the rule works well (particularly in the case of the UK), thus providing a cheapness or expensiveness indicator for the markets. When the sum of the two variables is well short of 20, shares are cheap; when it is comfortably clear of 20, they are expensive.

It should be no surprise that the rule has credibility. If the inflation rate rises, interest rates are likely to follow suit, thus driving down the price first of BONDS and then of equities. In other words, the market's P/E ratio will fall to compensate for the higher rate of inflation. Conversely, falling inflation and falling interest rates usually go together, signalling higher share prices. This is partly because low interest rates mean investors are willing to accept lower running returns and will therefore pay more for shares; and partly because they see more of their future returns coming from the higher share values which will flow from the increased economic activity engendered by low inflation.

The rule's limitation is that it assumes that future market movements will be based on indicators of past performance; whereas in reality a sum of over 20 may be perfectly reasonable if, for example, a high inflation rate is expected to fall fast, bringing with it a rapid upturn in real corporate profits.

S&P 500 Index

The benchmark index for large cap STOCKS in the United States run by Standard & Poor's, a financial information provider. Its constituents are shares in 500 companies each with a market capitalisation of at least $4 billion. As at the end of September 2008, its value was just over $10 trillion and the average market value of each company was £20 billion. It is a market value index, which means that its value is weighted by the stockmarket value of its constituents. A 1% change in the value of ExxonMobil, its biggest component, therefore, would have a greater impact than a 1% change in the value of Apple. Although it was started in 1957, the S&P's base value is 10 for the period 1941–43.

Sarbanes-Oxley Act

In 2002, in response to the trauma of big company failures and alleged dishonesty within corporate America – most notably at Enron, an energy trader, and WorldCom, a telecoms operator – President Bush signed the Sarbanes-Oxley Act, which he called "the most far-reaching reforms of American business practice since the times of Franklin Delano Roosevelt". He was not exaggerating. The act, named after Senator Paul Sarbanes and Congressman Mike Oxley, toughens US corporate governance in three main areas:

- New, and quicker, disclosure of information to the SECURITIES AND EXCHANGE COMMISSION (SEC). In particular, company chief executives and chief financial officers must certify the accuracy of their companies' financial statements, and the penalty for false disclosure can be imprisonment for up to 20 years. If there is a need to re-state company accounts, bosses may also have to repay their companies any bonus-related pay, including profits from selling STOCK OPTIONS, they received.

- New rules for companies' audit committees, which are responsible for various aspects of company financial reporting. In particular, all members of a company's audit committee must be independent of the company and there should be at least one finance expert on the committee; the company's auditor will report to the committee, which must approve any non-audit work to be done by the auditor.
- The establishment of a Public Company Accounting Oversight Board, which will be the federal watchdog for the auditing profession. In particular, the board will set standards with which auditing firms must comply; it will inspect them, investigate them and, where necessary, discipline them.

Since its introduction Sarbanes-Oxley has been controversial. In particular, its critics say the cost of complying with it has been far higher than expected and has outweighed its benefits. Moreover, the costs may have weakened US stockmarkets by encouraging foreign firms to list their shares in countries other than the United States and the bosses of smaller US companies to sell their businesses to PRIVATE EQUITY. It is also possible that the act has discouraged risk-taking by US companies.

However, these claims are difficult to prove mainly because of the problem of separating the effects of Sarbanes-Oxley from the effects of other measures introduced around the same time. Besides, following pressure from the SEC, changes to compliance procedures introduced in 2007 have made Sarbanes-Oxley less expensive.

Scrip issue

An arrangement largely confined to the UK, in which a company will CAPITALISE some of its retained EARNINGS. It is purely a book-keeping exercise in which a lump of capital is moved from one part of shareholders' EQUITY to another. Say the equity in a company looks like this:

	£m
Ordinary shares (25p par value)	200
Retained earnings	600
Unrealised revaluations	400
Total	**1,200**

Then the directors of the company decide on a capitalisation issue of one for two (that is, for every two shares that shareholders own, they receive one new share). The transfer would have to come from retained earnings, which would mean issuing another 400m shares with a 25p par value and switching the £100m needed to "pay" for the shares from retained earnings to ORDINARY SHARES. Thus after the exercise shareholders' equity would look like this:

	£m
Ordinary shares (25p par value)	300
Retained earnings	500
Unrealised revaluations	400
Total	**1,200**

It is important to realise that value has been neither created nor destroyed by the exercise. A shareholder with 10,000 shares in the company before the scrip issue would have a pro-rata claim on £120,000 of its NET WORTH. After the issue the shareholder's claim would still be £120,000; it would simply be divided among 15,000 shares and the per share value would have declined by one-third. Exactly the same would happen to the market value of the company's shares. If they traded at 600p each before the issue, they would, other things being equal, fall to 400p afterwards.

However, this caveat provides the justification for scrip issues. Some research indicates that share prices perform well immediately after such an issue – possibly because the liquidity of the company's stock has improved, thus helping some investors to buy, or, more tenuously, simply by making the share price look more attractive because it is lower. The latter explanation does not stand up to examination, but this does not stop some interested parties claiming it, particularly those company bosses who describe such an issue as a BONUS ISSUE.

SEAQ

See STOCK EXCHANGE AUTOMATED QUOTATIONS.

SEC

See next entry.

Securities and Exchange Commission

The watchdog that regulates the US securities industry. Like regulatory authorities in so many areas it is under-resourced, yet it has considerable powers and frequently uses them, most notably in recent years in the prosecution of Michael Milken and Ivan Boesky on insider dealing charges (see JUNK BOND). Both men got prison sentences; Milken was fined \$200m and ordered to pay \$400m into a restitution fund, and Boesky was fined \$100m. This is not bad for an organisation whose first chairman was Joseph P. Kennedy (father of John F.), a notorious inside trader in the 1920s when such practices were not illegal. Indeed, the Securities and Exchange Commission (SEC) was established in 1934 in response to Wall Street's excesses in the 1920s. It derives its powers from the Securities Act 1933, which governs the issue of securities to the public, and the Securities Exchange Act 1934, which regulates stock exchanges (including OPTIONS markets) and all those whose work is connected to them.

> *I want you to know that I think greed is healthy.*
> *You can be greedy and feel good about yourselves.*
> Ivan Boesky, to a class of business graduates at University of California

Securitisation

A means to turn illiquid assets into liquid ones, which has created a market worth perhaps $2 trillion in the United States alone. A typical securitisation deal takes a package of ASSETS – for example, MORTGAGES – and puts them into a SPECIAL PURPOSE VEHICLE (SPV). The SPV then issues tradable securities, which are secured against its portfolio of mortgages and which offer investors a stream of revenue that is generated from the regular payments of interest and principal that borrowers make.

For lenders (mostly banks), the chief benefit of securitisation is that it generates a lump sum of cash that can be used to do further business, rather than a stream of income stretching far into the future. For investors – the institutions that buy the asset-backed securities – securitised assets offer the likelihood of higher returns for a given level of RISK than conventional BONDS. That is because they are backed by a diversified portfolio of loans.

The history of securitisation dates back to 1970 when the US Department of Housing and Urban Development created the Government National Mortgage Association – or Ginnie Mae – which sold securities backed by portfolios of mortgages for house purchase. Since then securitisation has been used on many classes of loans that are otherwise illiquid but which have predictable cash flows – for example, loans for car purchase, student loans and credit-card receivables, and even future royalties due to rock singer David Bowie.

Security Analysis

Before Benjamin GRAHAM and David Dodd published *Security Analysis* in 1934 there was no formal analysis of the STOCKS and BONDS that trade on the US capital markets. Now security analysis is a quasi-science with all the attendant jargon (although, happily, the book is not responsible for this). There is the CFA Institute (formerly the Institute of Chartered Financial Analysts) primarily in the United States, the European Federation of Financial Analysts in the European Union, and the Securities & Investment Institute in the UK, which together have tens of thousands of members. The book, meanwhile, has been in print continuously since first being published. It remains a standard and down-to-earth work on the subject and is now into its sixth edition, which came out in 2008.

Security market line

The chart line that illustrates the idea that investors are rewarded only for the risks they take in relation to overall market risk (SYSTEMATIC RISK). As such, it is the linear representation of the CAPITAL ASSET PRICING MODEL.

Self-invested personal pension

This type of personal pension plan, abbreviated to SIPP, came into operation in the UK in 2001 and gives savers for retirement the option to invest in a wider range of ASSETS than a conventional pension plan allows. As well as permitting investment in listed shares, investment trusts and unit trusts, the rules controlling

SIPPs allow investment in FUTURES and OPTIONS that are traded on a recognised futures exchange, traded endowment policies and commercial property. Originally the UK government intended to allow SIPP money to be invested in bullion, residential property and exotic assets, such as wines and stamps. However, in a U-turn, the government imposed tax penalties that meant investment in such assets is no longer sensible.

Serious Fraud Office

A UK government department that pursues major fraud cases. It was established in 1988 and operates under powers in the 1987 Criminal Justice Act with a brief to investigate major and complex fraud cases where there is a public interest and the alleged fraud exceeds £1m. Although the Serious Fraud Office (SFO) has been criticised following the failure of some of its high-profile cases, over its first 20 years its conviction rate was 69% of the defendants it brought to trial. In the five years 2003–08, there were 67 trials involving 166 defendants, of whom 102 were found guilty, a conviction rate of 61%.

SETS

See STOCK EXCHANGE TRADING SERVICE.

SFO

See SERIOUS FRAUD OFFICE.

Sharpe ratio

Named after William Sharpe, who won a Nobel Prize for his work on financial economics, the Sharpe ratio measures the amount of return from an investment portfolio for a given level of RISK. It does this by dividing a measure of portfolio VOLATILITY (the STANDARD DEVIATION of its returns over a specific period) into the excess returns generated by the portfolio over the RISK-FREE RATE OF RETURN for the same period. The higher the resulting number, the better is the portfolio performance. This ratio, also known as the reward-to-variability ratio, is used to rank the performance of investment funds.

Short

The adjective that describes traders who have a position in a security that they do not own. In other words, they have committed to deliver STOCK at a specific price some time in the future and must buy in stock to fulfil their bargain. By definition therefore someone who is short of stock anticipates a fall in its price and is a BEAR (see LONG).

Short interest ratio

A measure of investor sentiment towards US common STOCKS, which is calculated monthly. It takes the total number of shares that have been sold SHORT and divides it by the market's average daily trading volume for the previous month. In other words, it expresses the number of days it will take for the market to work off its short position. The higher the ratio – the greater the number of days needed – the more bullish are the market's short-term prospects. This is so because, even though the stocks were sold short in the hope of a fall in the market, whatever happens they have to be bought back in order to close out the short-sale contracts. Thus the ratio is an indicator of latent demand in the market. Investors' ability to HEDGE short positions using FUTURES or OPTIONS means that the ratio has less relevance nowadays than in the past; even so, a ratio of above 4.0 for the NEW YORK STOCK EXCHANGE would be at the high end of the normal range and, therefore, a bullish signal.

Short selling

Selling something you do not own in the hope of buying it more cheaply in the future, thus making a profit. On the main US stock exchanges short selling remains popular and often accounts for approaching 10% of all bargains done on the NEW YORK STOCK EXCHANGE (although about half of this is generally done by specialists to meet buy orders). However, it is circumscribed by tight rules, in particular that short sales in a STOCK can be made only when the stock's most recent price change was up. Short sales are effected by borrowing stock from another party who still receives any dividends paid on the stock while the short sale remains in effect. Brokers require the seller to put up security against the sale, which is marked to market.

In the UK short sales used to be popular when shares were traded over a two-week accounting period for settling stock transactions. The abolition of these accounting periods effectively made short sales impractical, except for MARKETMAKERS, who sell short as part of their regular business. Besides, increasingly nowadays there are alternative ways of achieving short positions without selling short, such as using a PUT OPTION or a CONTRACT FOR DIFFERENCE.

Single index model

The trouble with PORTFOLIO THEORY when it was formulated was that prodigious amounts of calculation were needed in order to find those portfolios of investments that provided the best trade-offs between RISK and return. This was because the key measure of risk was how far the returns on each pair of investments in a portfolio varied in relation to each other. The groundwork for a portfolio of 200 stocks, for example, would need 19,900 COVARIANCE calculations.

However, it became increasingly clear that in the real world of stockmarkets much of the price changes in a security depended on movements in the whole market, so a portfolio model was developed which related returns on shares to their sensitivity to a single market index, say the S&P 500 INDEX of US stocks or London's ALL-SHARE INDEX. Basically, the single index model says that a security's return will comprise an independent return made irrespective of the market's returns plus the degree to which the security's own returns magnify or minimise the market's returns.

Say the independent return, called the share's ALPHA, was 8% a year, the market's return was 10% and the share's sensitivity to the market was 1.5 (that is, the share's returns were on average 1.5 times the market's, up or down). Then the share could be expected to return 23% if the market rose 10%, but just 0.5% if the market fell 5%. The calculations are a bit more complicated than this, as the formula in Appendix 5 shows. But the single index model works well and greatly reduces the work needed to find the best combinations of shares. For the same portfolio of 200 shares there would need to be only 602 calculations.

Sinking fund

The provision set aside for the repayment of a debt, most likely a marketable BOND. When the provision has been built up to sufficient levels the borrower can buy in the debt in the market. Effectively, therefore, the debt is paid off in instalments, giving the borrower greater flexibility. For the lenders (that is, those who own the bonds) the possibility of default is reduced.

SIPP

See SELF-INVESTED PERSONAL PENSION.

Small cap stock

Market shorthand for companies that have low stockmarket capitalisations. Small cap stocks are interesting because research in both the UK and the United States has shown that they produce better returns than bigger companies. As a rule of thumb, the excess returns increase as the market capitalisations get smaller. But because companies with low market capitalisations also often have a low share price, it is not always clear if the excess returns result from the market capitalisation or the share price. Studies have shown that both characteristics generate above-average returns.

It is more relevant to ask why this phenomenon persists even though it is well known. EFFICIENT MARKET HYPOTHESIS says that the extra returns should be priced away by profit-maximising investors. However, it is likely that the market is not particularly efficient at pricing small companies because it is not worthwhile for investment analysts to do the research on them that would produce a "correct" price. They may be more risky than big companies, although this does not show from the STANDARD DEVIATION of their returns. They may also carry greater risk of business failure as they are more vulnerable to swings in the economic cycle. Indeed, research into UK small cap stocks showed that their returns were well correlated with overall profits in the economy.

Soros, George

The man who famously "broke" the Bank of England when he took a massive position against sterling in 1992, thus helping to force the UK government out of a semi-fixed exchange rate mechanism with its EU partners. George Soros, a Hungarian-born New Yorker, set up the Quantum Fund, an offshore HEDGE FUND, which produced remarkable annual COMPOUND RETURNS of over 30% between 1969 and 1999. His style was to take big, often interlinked, speculative positions using lots of LEVERAGE so that, say, a 1% favourable move in the yen would produce a 10% gain in the fund's NET WORTH. This approach sometimes caused the Quantum Fund to sustain savage losses. For example, it lost 32% after the stockmarket crash of October 1987.

> *I was as badly caught as the next fellow. I was convinced the crash would start in Japan; that turned out to be an expensive mistake.*
> George Soros on the October 1987 crash, from *The Alchemy of Finance*

Sortino ratio

A variation on the SHARPE RATIO, named after Frank Sortino, an American academic. The major shortcoming of the Sharpe ratio is that it uses the STANDARD DEVIATION of a portfolio's returns as the yardstick against which excess returns are measured. However, standard deviation, which effectively measures the extent to which returns on average vary from their mean, treats above-average returns just the same as below-average ones, and this runs counter to most people's intuitive assessment of RISK. The Sortino ratio gets round this by using downside deviation as its measure of risk. Thus, in a series of portfolio returns, downside deviation ignores – that is, gives a value of zero to – all returns that are above average and calculates the standard deviation of just the below-average returns. Put formally, it takes as its numerator portfolio returns minus a target return and as its denominator downside deviation. So it calculates excess returns per unit of downside risk. The higher the number the better, though the Sortino ratio has value only as a tool for comparing the performance of portfolios – it offers no absolute scale of good or bad.

South Sea Bubble

One of the earliest, and arguably most infamous, episodes of share speculation gone mad. It featured the South Sea Company, a London company whose aim was to trade in Spanish South America in the early 18th century and whose confidence of success was such that it offered to swap all the British government's debt for its own shares. Encouraged by the British government, which was apprehensive that the French government was in the process of getting rid of its own debt by a similarly fraudulent scheme and therefore keen to do the same, and lapped up by a newly wealthy British public, South Sea Company shares surged from around £100 at the start of 1720 to £307 when the law was passed permitting the takeover of the national debt. Stimulated by further issues of partly paid shares at £300 and £400, the South Sea shares rose to £1,050 by June 24th 1720. By then rumours that the company's directors were selling leaked out. Coupled with the dawning realisation that the company's trading prospects were non-existent, the shares plummeted to £150 by the end of September.

Special purpose vehicle

Better known as a special purpose entity (SPE) in the United States, this is a corporation that has been set up for a specific purpose, most often to isolate financial RISK. Thus, for example, a bank that wants to raise capital by issuing MORTGAGE-backed securities, whose interest payments will come from a pool of mortgages, would isolate those mortgages in a special purpose vehicle (SPV). By arranging its finances this way, the securitised loans would not count as part of the bank's assets for regulatory purposes, leaving it free to make more loans than would be the case without the SPV.

Specialist

See MARKETMAKER.

Speculative value

See TIME VALUE.

Speculator

A term of abuse directed at a market's participants when markets move in ways that are both strange and disadvantageous to the general public. More specifically, speculators perform a useful function. For a price they will assume RISK, much like an insurance company assumes the potential cost of a domestic mishap. In so doing, they also maintain a market's liquidity by buying when there is a surfeit of sellers and supplying the market's stock-in-trade when buyers are abundant.

Spot price

The price of an ASSET for immediate delivery; that is, as soon as the delivery mechanism used between the buyer and seller allows. It is usually used in the currency or commodity markets to distinguish between the price of goods for immediate delivery and the price for delivery at a specific time in the future.

Spread

The difference between the price at which a marketable security is bought and sold. Thus it is the wholesaler's, or MARKETMAKER's, mark-up.

In OPTIONS trading, spread is the generic term that embraces a variety of strategies whose common characteristic is that the potential maximum profit and maximum loss are known at the outset of the transaction. This is because an investor places himself on both sides of the transaction and therefore, beyond certain movements in the price of the underlying STOCK, finds that the profits and losses from his positions cancel themselves out. Spread strategies fall into two categories:

- Money, or vertical, spreads where the investor takes advantage of the differing values given to options which have the same expiry date, but a different EXERCISE PRICE.
- Time, or horizontal, spreads where investors simultaneously buy and sell options contracts which are identical apart from their expiry dates, thus seeking to take advantage of the different rates at which TIME VALUE in options erodes.

For example, take a BULL call spread, the most popular variation on the theme. An investor buys a CALL OPTION with a low exercise price and simultaneously sells, or writes, a call option (that is, agrees to deliver stock) with the same expiry date but at a higher exercise price. The immediate effect is that he receives less premium income than the cost of the call he buys. But this would represent his maximum potential loss if the underlying stock price falls. This is so because if the stock price falls sufficiently he would not want to exercise his right to buy stock, but nor would he have to deliver stock at an even higher exercise price. If, however, the stock rises as hoped the call option would become increasingly valuable, but the profit derived from it would be pegged by the losses that would ensue from the call the investor had written at the higher exercise price.

> *It's not whether you are right or wrong that's important, but how much money you make when you're right and how much you lose when you're wrong.*
>
> George Soros, Hungarian-born financier and philanthropist

Spread betting

A means to add RISK to a portfolio or to reduce it which also offers the possibility to gamble on almost anything that can be quantified. For example, in early 2003, among London's MARKETMAKERS it was possible to place a spread bet on the amount of time that the chief executive of a deeply troubled FTSE 100 company would remain in his job. Marketmakers were quoting 40–42 days, so anyone who thought that the poor man would not last 40 days – the BEARS – would "sell" the wager at 40. Those who thought he would last more than 42 days – the BULLS – would "buy" at 42. If, say, the boss lasted 45 days before his dismissal, the buyers at 42 would have made a profit of three days multiplied by their wager per day (three times £100, for instance). The bears would have to settle their obligation to sell the wager at 40 days by buying in at 45 days. In other words, they would have lost five days multiplied by their wager per day.

Meanwhile, the aim of the marketmaker would be to maintain a balance between buyers and sellers. If successful, he would have no net exposure to the wager and would pocket the spread between the buy and sell prices he was quoting. In that sense, spread betting is no different from what a marketmaker does in a listed security; nor is it much different from the CONTRACTS FOR DIFFERENCE that many companies enter into to limit their exposure to a particular cost (the cost of wholesale electricity to an electricity supplier, for example).

Stag

Someone who buys shares in a new issue with the intention of selling for a profit as soon as dealings in the market begin.

Standard deviation

The statistical measure without which PORTFOLIO THEORY would not be as we know it today. The great merit of standard deviation is that it measures variations around an average in a way that is accessible to everyone. Take, for example, the performance figures for the world's leading stockmarkets. These show that from 1968 to 2008 the average annual change in the value of the DOW JONES INDUSTRIAL AVERAGE was 6% and for the FTSE ALL-SHARE INDEX it was 7%. On this basis, ignoring, for argument's sake, the effects of exchange rates, an investor would have preferred to have had a long-term holding in the All-Share Index.

However, the standard deviation of the All-Share at 29% was almost twice as high as the Dow, whose standard deviation was 17%. This puts a different complexion on things. Given that a normal distribution pattern shows that two-thirds of the time returns will be within plus or minus one standard deviation of the average, then two out of three of the All-Share's returns would have been within 36% and –22% and two-thirds of the Dow's would been within 24% and –12%.

Thus using standard deviation tells us that an investor who is reluctant to live with the possibility of uncomfortably large annual losses in return for the potential for big annual gains would prefer the comparatively quiet life offered by the Dow's returns. Given that portfolio theory is all about the trade-off between RISK and returns, standard deviation becomes a useful measure – more useful, incidentally, than VARIANCE, the statistical measure from which it is derived. Variance expresses deviation from the average in terms of the square of the unit measured, whereas standard deviation, which is the square root of variance, talks in terms of the actual units.

Stock

A little word that is full of ambiguous meaning:

- In the UK it is often used as an abbreviation for GILT-EDGED STOCK and thence an abbreviation for all types of FIXED INTEREST SECURITY.
- Additionally in the UK it is used as a substitute for security.
- In the United States it is used as an abbreviation for COMMON STOCK.
- Within a company's BALANCE SHEET, stock is the old word for INVENTORY, that is, the goods which a company processes in the expectation of making a profit.

> *They told me to buy this stock for my old age. It worked wonderfully. Within a week I was an old man.*
> Eddie Cantor

Stockbroker

The agent who buys and sells quoted securities on behalf of his clients and in return is paid a commission based on the value of the business done. As an agent the broker has a legal obligation to transact the business at the best possible price for the client. Increasingly, however, stockbrokers perform an array of functions, all related to investing in quoted securities. This may include fund management (managing clients' investment portfolios) and trustee services (looking after all the financial needs of wealthy clients). Most of the world's major investment banks have stockbroking arms. In the case of some (for example, Merrill Lynch in the United States and Nomura in Japan) the bank grew out of the broking arm. In other cases (for example, Banque Paribas in France) a broking arm was added to help distribute the securities generated from INVESTMENT BANKING functions.

> *'Tis a compleat system of knavery, that 'tis a trade founded in fraud, born of deceit and nourished by trick, cheat, wheedle, forgeries, falsehoods and all sorts of delusions.*
>
> Daniel Defoe on stockbroking

Stock Exchange Automated Quotations

The key trading platform on the LONDON STOCK EXCHANGE when it was introduced as part of BIG BANG in 1986. Now, however, the Stock Exchange Automated Quotations system (SEAQ – pronounced "see-ack") is a marginal part of London's securities-trading platform and the remaining segment where MARKETMAKERS exclusively supply price quotations. A few securities that are floated on London's ALTERNATIVE INVESTMENT MARKET and FIXED-INTEREST SECURITIES are still traded on the SEAQ platform.

Stock Exchange Trading Service

Known as SETS, this is the main securities trading platform of the LONDON STOCK EXCHANGE, which is based on a public limit order book where all market participants can post price and size limits on securities in which they want to deal. The order book is supplemented by MARKETMAKERS, who guarantee the provision of liquidity in the most widely traded stocks. Shares in all the constituents of the FTSE ALL-SHARE INDEX are traded on SETS as are about 180 of the most liquid securities on the ALTERNATIVE INVESTMENT MARKET and EXCHANGE TRADED FUNDS that have their listing in London. SETS was introduced in 1997 and was originally confined to the biggest and most liquid issues. Its early years were a disappointment. The system did not bring the price competition hoped for and was investigated by the UK's competition authorities. Now, however, the problems are forgotten.

Stop loss

On the logic that any stockmarket investment has an element of gambling, a stop loss is a sensible and simple tactic which, if adhered to, will almost always limit losses in any situation. All it entails is an instruction to sell a security if its price falls below a pre-defined level. The major risk it carries is that in a chaotic market the stop-loss order may not be capable of execution near the level specified. Additionally, there is the potential for an opportunity loss if the security's price subsequently recovers. Even so, in high-risk OPTIONS and FUTURES strategies, a stop loss is a prerequisite.

> “ *It requires a great deal of boldness and a great deal of caution to make a great fortune.*
> Nathan Mayer Rothschild

Straddle

A tactic used in OPTIONS trading which would be employed by someone who expects the price of underlying shares to be volatile. Investors simultaneously buy a CALL OPTION and a PUT OPTION in a share which have the same EXERCISE PRICE and expiry date. Thus they can make money if the share price rises or falls. However, for them to profit, the share price has to move further in at least one direction than if they were just buying a call or a put. This is because they have to cover the cost of two contracts. Thus their break-even position has been extended.

Someone on the other side of the transaction must believe that the underlying share price will move little during the period of the contract. He simultaneously sells both a call and a put and, in market jargon, has written a "SHORT straddle". The advantage to the WRITER of the short straddle is that he receives two lots of premium income. Against that, he can lose money on both the call and the put if the price turns out to be especially volatile. In practice, he would probably have a STOP LOSS position on one side of the transaction to limit the potential losses in one direction.

Strike price

See EXERCISE PRICE.

Strips

It seems common sense that if an investment bank strips the coupons from a BOND and sells them separately, the word "strips" self-evidently describes the product. However, when the US Treasury launched its version of stripped bonds it felt obliged to make an acronym of the word. Hence strips now stands for Separate Trading of Registered Interest and Principal of Securities. Take, for example, a 15-year TREASURY BOND. It could be carved up into 30 discounted securities, each of which would represent a claim on a future interest payment, and a 31st, which would be a claim on the principal on redemption. Effectively, therefore, 31 ZERO-COUPON BONDS would have been created, offering investors almost any maturity and all free from risk of default.

Strips were, in fact, the Treasury's response to an unofficial market in stripped government bonds. Merrill Lynch, an investment bank, led the way with TIGRS (or Tigers), Treasury Investment Growth Receipts; Salomon Brothers, another bank, followed with CATS, Certificates of Accrual on Treasury Securities; and so the market (and the acronyms) grew. The success of bond stripping even persuaded the Bank of England to launch an official market into stripped GILT-EDGED STOCK, which began in 1997.

Survivor bias

Jargon for the unwarranted statistical importance given to the performance of survivors in a process. Within the context of investment, the returns of those shares or stockmarkets that have survived colour investors' expectations too much. So, for example, the 20th century's EQUITY returns for the United States and UK combined averaged about 8% a year before the effect of DIVIDENDS. The figure is interpreted as one that has stood the test of time and all the vicissitudes that life can throw its way and will, therefore, apply in the long term, too. To assume that, however, would be to fall for survivor bias. The 8% annual return ignores the impact of, say, the wipe-out of Russian stocks in 1917 and German bonds in the 1920s. Factor in the effect of the markets that did not survive and overall investment returns might be very different. Similarly, most major stockmarket indices display survivor bias because they exclude those stocks whose value falls below a specified threshold in favour of those which have crossed the threshold – that is, they systematically favour the survivors.

Swaps

A DERIVATIVES product; a way in which borrowers or lenders of funds remove either the interest rate risk or the exchange rate risk, or both, from a transaction. Thus a company which had variable rate borrowings could remove its exposure to a rise in interest rates by arranging with a bank to swap its floating-rate payments for a fixed-rate payment, although clearly in doing so it is actually swapping one sort of RISK for another. The variations on the theme are enormous, including being able to buy the OPTION to take out a swap within a specific period: a swaption.

Systematic risk

If RISK is the possibility that investment returns will fail to reach expectations, then systematic risk comprises those components of overall risk that cannot be eliminated by allocating capital to a diversified portfolio of investments. Primarily this consists of market risk. An investment in a particular market must necessarily bear those risks that affect the whole market; if a stockmarket falls, most of the stocks that trade within it will suffer to some extent. Closely related to market risk is interest rate risk. Clearly, the short-term values of many investments will be depressed if interest rates rise. Similarly, the risk of inflation – the declining purchasing power of invested money – is difficult to escape. (See also UNSYSTEMATIC RISK.)

The Takeover Panel

The UK's regulatory body that is concerned with the takeover of companies whose shares are held by the public. The panel was set up in 1968 in response to growing criticism of unfair takeover practices. Its brief is to ensure that all shareholders in a company in receipt of a takeover bid are treated fairly, according to the City Code of Takeovers and Mergers. Although it has no sanctions of its own, the panel's reputation for dispensing common-sense rulings speedily during the hurly-burly of a takeover means that it is a successful example of self-regulation.

Tax-exempt special savings account

The bottom rung of the tax-free savings and investment ladder in the UK introduced in 1991. A tax-exempt special savings account (TESSA) allowed anyone aged over 18 to earn interest tax-free from a savings account, provided they stuck to a few rules. The most important was that within specific annual limits no more than £9,000 could be deposited over the TESSA's five-year term. Tessas were abolished in 1999 and replaced by the INDIVIDUAL SAVINGS ACCOUNT (ISA) scheme. However, the capital sum originally invested in a TESSA can still be rolled over into a TESSA-only ISA.

TechMARK

A stockmarket within a stockmarket, techMARK was created by the LONDON STOCK EXCHANGE in November 1999 to give a streamlined listing procedure for companies within supposedly high-growth technology sectors, with a particular focus on medical sciences since the dotcom bubble burst. Most techMARK companies are small, with a market capitalisation of under £50m, although the market includes some constituents of the FTSE 100 and FTSE 250 indices. As at end-March 2008, there were 114 techMARK companies with a combined market value of £265 billion, compared with a value of over £650 billion when the market was at its 2000 peak.

Technical analysis

The branch of investment analysis that is sometimes ridiculed, yet survives and at times thrives. It is ridiculed because it is easy to grasp and requires no great intellectual effort. It survives because – who knows? – it might just work and it almost certainly helps give insights into the psychology of investors in a particular market.

The basic idea of technical analysis is that it makes price predictions based on published data – mostly prices, but also volume of business done – of a STOCK, commodity, market, whatever. By looking at past price/volume patterns and applying rules of thumb, "buy" and "sell" signals are generated for the present. It readily follows, therefore, that most technical analysis is done using charts because of the ease with which they can show trends. Consequently, technical analysts are referred to as CHARTISTS.

Technical analysis assumes that market prices are driven by factors which have more to do with the psychology of a market's participants than with changes in underlying economic values. Therefore it searches for trends, which are often self-reinforcing, and for signs of the tensions that mount before trends are broken. Support and resistance levels for a price thus become important.

Many investment analysts who ridicule technical analysis

unknowingly use technical techniques in their analysis; the ubiquity of computer-generated price charts ensures this. However, the credibility of technical analysis has never really been the same since the development in the 1960s of the EFFICIENT MARKET HYPOTHESIS and RANDOM WALK theory. Few people believe that even big, liquid markets are truly efficient, although there is a lot of evidence to show that they are efficient enough to render unobtainable on a consistent basis the excess profits that technical analysts claim can be generated from predicting future prices on the basis of past price patterns.

Term

The length of time until the specific date when a BOND matures; that is, the principal is repaid.

Term structure of interest rates

The relationship between the maturity of notes and bonds and the interest rates they offer. Several theories are advanced about this, all of which have some use.

Expectations theory. The interest rate on a long-term BOND will equal the average of rates on a succession of short-term bonds, assuming all the bonds pay the same COUPON. So the interest rate on a three-year bond would be the average of the known rate for a one-year bond plus the implied rates for bonds which become one-year instruments at the start of years two and three. This sounds unnecessarily complex, but the implication is that someone who wants to buy a three-year bond might just as well buy a succession of three one-year bonds, or buy a five-year bond and sell it after three years. The result should be the same. The trouble is that there can only be the implication, and never the certainty, that future rates will come to pass. So people who want to invest for, say, three years through buying a succession of three one-year bonds face risks each time they have to switch bonds.

Liquidity preference theory. Lenders prefer to lend for the short term and borrowers prefer to borrow for the long term. So lenders get a premium to be persuaded to lend LONG and borrowers receive a discount for borrowing SHORT. Thus the theory acknowledges RISK in a way that expectations theory does not and explains why the YIELD CURVE should slope upwards.

Market segmentation theory. Particular types of investors focus their activities in particular maturity segments of the market. Banks invest in short-term bonds. Life insurers invest long because they have long-term liabilities they can identify well in advance. Those areas of the market for which there are few natural investors are fairly friendless, so interest rates there are higher. It is a useful theory in so far as it helps explain why the yield curve is often humped around some maturities.

“ *In investing money, the amount of interest you want should depend on whether you want to eat well or sleep well.*

J. Kenfield Morley, *Some Things I Believe*

TESSA

See TAX-EXEMPT SPECIAL SAVINGS ACCOUNT.

Tick

The smallest price move that a market's regulations will allow in a financial product that the market trades. The term is primarily confined to the currencies and FUTURES markets. On London's futures market, EURONEXT.LIFFE, for example, the tick size on the

FTSE 100 INDEX contract is half a point; that is, from 3810.0 to 3810.5 or 3809.5. In the LONG gilts contract it is £0.03 and in interest rate contracts it is one basis point; that is, one-hundredth of a percentage point.

Time value

One of the core tenets of investment – and, indeed, capitalism – that money has a time value, meaning that money received in the present is intrinsically more valuable than money received in the future. It is the economic expression of the "bird in the hand" proverb, and to calculate what the "two in the bush" are worth an appropriate DISCOUNT RATE must be used. In other words, if an investor's expected rate of return is 10% per year, then clearly that investor would reject the offer of £109 in a year's time instead of £100 today, would be indifferent about receiving £110 in a year or £100 today and would accept £111 one year hence in preference to £100 today.

In options, time value is one of the two components of the price that investors pay to acquire an OPTION to buy or sell a STOCK at a specific price at some point in the future. Time value equals the price of the option (the PREMIUM, to use the jargon) minus the option's INTRINSIC VALUE. If a stock currently trades at 95p and if the market price of the right, but not the obligation, to buy the stock on or before a specific date at 90p is currently 8p, that price comprises 5p of intrinsic value and 3p of time value. The intrinsic value derives from the fact that the price at which the option can be exercised is 5p less than the market price. The time value is the residual amount and is what the buyer pays for the privilege of being able to make profits during the time until the option expires; and that will primarily depend on price movements in the underlying security.

Time value is also known as speculative value.

Tobin's Q

Named after James Tobin, a Yale academic, "Q" measures the ratio of the stockmarket value of the debt and EQUITY that a company employs to the replacement cost of the company's tangible ASSETS. Thus a ratio above 1 would attract capital into building assets because those assets would be valued at more than their cost by the market. For a ratio below 1, it would be more profitable to build businesses by acquisition than by capital spending. Tobin's Q has little meaning when applied to individual companies. However, when applied to a stockmarket as a whole it indicates cheapness or expensiveness. That said, as companies in the developed economies increasingly spend more on RESEARCH AND DEVELOPMENT per dollar of revenue and less on tangible assets, it is debatable whether a ratio of above 1 has as much predictive value as it seemed to do in the 1960s and 1970s.

Tokyo Stock Exchange

When Japanese share prices peaked at the end of 1989, the Tokyo Stock Exchange eclipsed the NEW YORK STOCK EXCHANGE as the world's biggest, as measured by the market capitalisation of listed securities. Happy days. Since then the main index of Japanese shares, the NIKKEI 225, has fallen by around 75%. Even so, the Tokyo exchange, which was established in 1878 and is one of five stock exchanges in Japan, is still the world's second biggest exchange by market capitalisation. At the end of 2008 its market value was $3,116 billion. Of this, 98% was concentrated in its "first section" of shares in 1,700 or so bigger companies. The Tokyo exchange also has a second section of shares in about 500 mid-sized companies and a so-called Mother's section of shares in 150 or so smaller, though hopefully fast-growing, companies.

In April 1999 floor trading of shares was scrapped. Since then, trading – and settlement – has been electronic. Orders are placed with Trading Participants, securities companies that act as brokers but also trade for their own account.

The exchange is structured as a joint stock company, although it has remained outside the rounds of takeover and merger that have included all other major stockmarkets. However, the Tokyo exchange did acquire a 5% interest in the Singapore Exchange in 2007 and has a technology sharing agreement with the LONDON STOCK EXCHANGE.

TOPIX

Shorthand for Tokyo Stock Price Index, the broadest measure of share values on the TOKYO STOCK EXCHANGE. It is an index of all stocks quoted on the "first section" of the Tokyo exchange (that is, about 1,700 larger issues). It measures changes in the market value of Tokyo stocks against a base value struck in 1969, after adjusting for factors such as the conversion of convertible securities. Arguably, therefore, it gives a more accurate measure of the value of the Tokyo exchange than the more widely quoted NIKKEI 225 Index.

Total return

The return from an investment that includes the effect of both income and changes in value over a specified period – usually expressed as percentage of market price or price paid by an investor. Imagine the price of an ORDINARY SHARE moves from 100p to 130p over the course of a calendar year. If the per-share DIVIDEND paid to shareholders during the year was 5p, the total return would be 35%. By the same principle, if the dividend was the same but the price of the shares fell from 100p to 97p during the year, the total return would be just 2%.

Touch

In the London stockmarket, jargon for the best BID PRICE and OFFER PRICE for a share quoted by competing MARKETMAKERS. For example, if many firms make a market in a leading company's shares, among them might be bids of anything between, say, 346p and 349p to buy the share and offers of anything from 351p to 354p to sell it. The touch in this case would be 349–351p, regardless of which and how many firms bid or offer the most competitive prices.

Tracker fund

UK terminology for INDEX FUND.

Traded option

See OPTION.

Trading collar

A means by which a stockmarket protects itself against potentially destabilising trades in its related OPTIONS or FUTURES markets. For example, on the NEW YORK STOCK EXCHANGE trading collars are instituted when on any trading day the NYSE COMPOSITE INDEX moves up or down by at least 2% from its previous day's close. If the NYSE Composite falls by 2%, then the collar requires all INDEX ARBITRAGE orders to sell stocks that are components of the S&P 500 INDEX to be at a price not lower than the previous sell price. If the NYSE Composite rises by 2%, the collar requires all buy orders to be at a price higher than the last sell price. Trading collars are removed if the index returns to within 1% of its previous day's close. The specific number of points change in the index needed to trigger a trading collar is set in January, April, June and October, based on the closing values of the index for the previous month.

Transaction costs

Much investment theory ignores transaction costs, assuming, as it does, perfect markets where information glides freely and the costs of buying and selling investments are zero. The trouble is the real world is not like that. Transaction costs add a significant amount to the cost of dealing and, therefore, affect the net returns available on investments. In well-developed stockmarkets the major transaction cost is often that of bearing the mark-up charged by wholesalers (MARKETMAKERS) who are almost always ready to deal in a STOCK. Behind this come agents' fees for carrying out the business, taxes on these fees and, quite possibly, a charge levied by the stock exchange itself to maintain its own infrastructure.

Treasury bill

A short-term debt instrument used by both US and UK central banks to raise money and, more importantly, to regulate interest rates. Treasury bills are discounted securities, meaning they are sold at less than face value and the return to buyers comes from their receiving face value of the bills on maturity. In the UK this is always 91 days after issue, but in the United States it may be after three, six or 12 months. Because the chances of either central bank defaulting on its repayment is just about zero, Treasury bills also function as a benchmark for the RISK-FREE RATE OF RETURN.

Treasury bond

A fixed-interest security used to meet the US Treasury's long-term funding needs. Treasury bonds have maturities of anything from ten to 30 years. As at December 31st 2008, $595 billion of these bonds were outstanding, representing about 10% of the Treasury's marketable debt. Treasury bonds are issued at par, with institutions bidding for them on a YIELD basis (the lower the bid, the higher is the yield). Interest on them is paid at six-monthly intervals.

Treasury note

With maturities on issue of anything between two and ten years, Treasury notes are the US Treasury's intermediate form of debt. Like TREASURY BONDS they are issued at par; unlike some Treasury bonds, however, they have only one specific maturity date and therefore can be used by some investors to match their assets with their liabilities. As at December 31st 2008, there were $2,792 billion of Treasury notes outstanding, representing about 48% of the Treasury's marketable debt.

“ *A national debt, if it be not excessive, will be a national blessing.*

Alexander Hamilton, the first US Treasury Secretary

Triple witching

In the United States, once every quarter – on the third Friday of March, June, September and December – contracts in traded OPTIONS, index options and FUTURES all expire simultaneously. This can give rise to frenetic trading as investors seek to balance their books, especially when the contracts all expired in the same hour, as used to be the case. Now, however, the authorities have arranged for contracts to expire at different times of the day, so reducing the potential for exaggerated VOLATILITY.

Tulipmania

A famous speculative bubble that took place in the Netherlands in the period 1634–37, during which time the price of best-quality tulip bulbs rose to the equivalent of $16,000 each. Tulips had been introduced into Europe from Turkey in the mid-1500s, but became fashionable among wealthy Dutch society in the early 17th century when diseased bulbs that produced unusually patterned flowers appeared. These could not be reproduced through seeds but only through budding the mother bulb, thus highly unusual bulbs may have had some propagative value. However, by late 1636 speculation spread to even common bulbs and the worst losses were suffered by those who had speculated in these. Prices of best-quality bulbs also fell rapidly, but possibly by no more than would have been expected as bulbs proliferated through propagation.

Unit trust

An investment vehicle with two different meanings depending on which side of the Atlantic you are situated.

- In the UK, a unit trust is the generic name for a MUTUAL FUND.
- In the United States, a unit trust – its full name is unit investment trust – is an unmanaged portfolio of ASSETS, usually BONDS, often with a fixed life in which units of, say, $1,000 a piece are sold. The assets generally remain unchanged. Although redemption of units is possible, it is more likely that the trust's sponsors will arrange a secondary market in units to avoid liquidating too much of the trust's portfolio.

Unsystematic risk

The investment risks that can be largely eliminated by holding a diversified portfolio of investments; the point being that separate factors will depress different investments at different times, thus changes in their value will not be synchronised. Within stockmarket investment, three factors cover most elements of unsystematic risk:

1 **Business risk.** Domestic and global economic cycles will influence individual companies differently. A sharp rise in commodity prices will benefit commodity producers, but companies that process commodities will simultaneously

suffer if they are caught by higher input prices which they cannot pass on to their customers.

2 **Financial risk.** Take one company operating with a great deal of debt in its BALANCE SHEET and another which has surplus cash. Other things being equal, their share prices would move in opposite directions if there were a marked rise in interest rates.

3 **Liquidity risk.** Some investments are easier to buy and sell than others because there is a ready market for them. Those which are difficult to trade (that is, have poor liquidity) are more vulnerable when values fall and therefore risky. In stockmarket terms, government bonds or TREASURY BILLS can almost always be traded and so have little liquidity risk. Conversely, the shares of companies which trade only on OVER-THE-COUNTER markets have a great deal of such risk.

Value investing

Caricatured as buying a dollar for 50 cents, or BOTTOM FISHING, value investing is a broad church that defies conventional definitions. It is more about a frame of mind than specific investment techniques and was best summed up by Benjamin GRAHAM when he coined the maxim "Margin of Safety" to encapsulate the value approach. By this he meant that there must be a substantial difference between the price paid for a share by an investor and the investor's assessment of its true value, even though the methods of assessing that value may vary widely. The popular image of value investors – that they seek out the shares of companies whose stockmarket value is less than the BALANCE SHEET value of their shareholders' EQUITY – is only partly true. For example, arguably today's best-known value investor, Warren BUFFETT, values companies on the fairly conventional assessment of the present value of their future cash flows. But to the extent that he insists on securing the margin of safety between what he is paying and what he is getting he is a value investor.

> *The greatest of all gifts is the power to estimate things at their true worth.*
>
> La Rochefoucauld, *Réflexions; ou sentences et maximes morales*

Value Line Composite Index

A wide-ranging index of north American stocks that comes in two variations. Both of them are unweighted for the market value of their components, which makes them unusual and arguably more representative of the portfolio performance of a typical private investor's portfolio.

The Value Line Composite Index was introduced in June 1961 when it was calculated as the GEOMETRIC MEAN of the unweighted daily price changes of its components. As such, the index – known as the VLG – provided an approximation of how the median stock in its universe of stocks performed. In 1988, its owner began to produce an index based on the ARITHMETIC MEAN of its components' daily price changes. This variation of the index – the VLA – produced returns that were more closely aligned to the returns of the other major US stockmarket indices and which, by definition, were more volatile than those of the VLG.

Both variations of the index are calculated from the same basket of approximately 1,600 stocks, all of which are listed on the major US stock exchanges with the exception of about 20 that are listed on the Toronto Stock Exchange.

Vanilla

The no-frills version of an investment. If it were a BOND, the plain vanilla version would be a standard FIXED-INCOME SECURITY issued at near par, paying half-yearly DIVIDENDS and maturing at a specific date when it would be repaid at par (that is, $100 would be repaid for every $100 nominal of STOCK). If it were a CLOSED-END FUND, its capital structure would simply comprise ORDINARY SHARES, which would have exclusive rights to both the stream of income from the company's investments and any capital gains.

Variance

A number that defines the extent to which a series of numbers are dispersed around (vary from) their average. It is a key component for measuring RISK in a security or a portfolio, where variance calculates how far an investment's returns for specific periods have varied from its average returns for the whole period under review. Basically, the bigger the number, the more volatile and, therefore, the riskier is the investment. The limitation of variance as a statistical measure is that it is expressed in terms of the square of the series of numbers involved, which is not always easy to grasp. The variance of returns on a portfolio, for example, would be in squares of percentages rather than just percentages. Hence the wider use of STANDARD DEVIATION as a basic measure of risk – because it is the square root of the variance, it measures dispersion in the same values as the average itself.

Venture capital

A type of PRIVATE EQUITY in which equity capital is invested in young companies which do not have the cash flows to support debt financing or the financial record to enable them to raise funds from a stock exchange, but which do have the potential to generate high growth. This implies high returns for the capital providers, but it comes with high risks of failure. Most venture capital is provided via funds that are structured as partnerships and run by general partners who are usually investment professionals or business people who can bring operational expertise to specific industries in which their funds invest. In the formative years of venture capital in the 1950s in the United States most capital was provided by wealthy people. Nowadays, however, capital providers – or limited partners – are increasingly investing institutions, such as pension funds.

Volatility

The propensity for the market price of an ASSET to bounce around. Volatility is a crucial factor in many of the arithmetic models that seek to justify current market prices or predict future ones. Since volatility equates to the variability of returns from an investment, it is an acceptable substitute for RISK; the greater the volatility, the greater is the risk that an investment will not turn out as hoped because its market price happens to be on the downswing of a bounce at the time that it needs to be cashed in. The problem is that future volatility is hard to predict and measures of past volatility can themselves be variable, depending on how frequently returns are measured (weekly or monthly, for example) and for how long. Therefore, putting expectations of future volatility into predictive models is of limited use, but resorting to using past levels of volatility is equally limited.

Yet two of the best-known and most widely used price models in investment analysis – the BLACK-SCHOLES OPTION PRICING MODEL and the CAPITAL ASSET PRICING MODEL – use a measure of volatility as the sole variable in their equations: STANDARD DEVIATION, which is a measure of absolute volatility, in the Black-Scholes model; and BETA, which measures relative volatility, in the CAP-M. This by no means renders these models useless, but it does mean their results should be treated with caution.

> *Volatility per se, be it related to weather, portfolio returns, or the timing of one's morning newspaper delivery, is simply a benign statistical probability factor that tells us nothing about risk until coupled with a consequence.*
>
> Robert H. Jeffrey

Wall Street Crash

There have been many crashes on Wall Street, with 1873, 1907, 1949 and 1987 prominent among them, but there has been only one Wall Street Crash. This epithet describes the period from September to November 1929 when the stockmarket, as measured by the DOW JONES INDUSTRIAL AVERAGE, fell 48% from its peak of 381.2 on September 3rd to 198.7 on November 13th. During these ten weeks there were two days – October 28th and 29th – when the industrial average fell 13.5% and 11.7% respectively. These were the two worst days in the history of the Dow after 1914 until BLACK MONDAY.

The background to the crash was a period of sustained easy money and rising prosperity, which propelled the market up. In an attempt to curb stockmarket speculation, the US banking authorities then raised interest rates aggressively. This succeeded in killing off the speculation but also dragged the US economy into what became the Great Depression. This, in turn, pulled the market down further till the industrial average bottomed out in July 1932, having lost 87% of its value from its September 1929 peak.

> “ *The stockmarket represents everything that anybody has ever hoped, feared or loved, it is all of life.*
>
> Edward C. Johnson II, owner of Fidelity Funds

Warrant

A warrant, much like a CALL OPTION, gives the holder the right, but not the obligation, to subscribe for ORDINARY SHARES almost always, although not necessarily, in the issuing company. The main differences compared with OPTIONS are that warrants have much longer maturities (typically anything from three to ten years) and are generally issued by a company and therefore raise new money for it. Over the years they have swung in and out of fashion, being much favoured by Japanese companies, which attached warrants to EUROBOND issues during the 1980s BULL market, and by UK investment trusts, which habitually attached them to new share issues in the 1980s. In both cases warrants functioned as a sweetener to the issue. This meant that in the case of Japanese Eurobonds, the issues could be sold at a lower interest rate than otherwise would have applied. Their function in UK investment trust (CLOSED-END FUND) issues was to close the discount to net asset value at which investment trust shares usually traded in the market.

When used as a sweetener, warrants are habitually, although misleadingly, referred to as "free". They seem to create value for shareholders because the warrants themselves have a market value which, when combined with the market value of the new shares, gives an overall increase in value. What is really happening is that the shareholders are being given tomorrow's jam today. Eventually the warrants will be converted into ordinary shares and have a claim on the company's assets, but if conversion is still far into the future that claim will probably not be recognised in the current share price. Hence the illusion of value created.

For anyone who doubts the illusion, consider the effect when the warrants are converted. Imagine that a company has net assets of 100p a share and issues warrants on a one-for-five basis to be converted in five years' time at 120p a share. Assume that during those five years the corporation's net assets grow at 15% a year. At the end of the period net assets would be 200p a share. But converting the warrants into shares at 120p each would have the effect of cutting net assets to 187p a share. Thus the DILUTION in the future equalises the "value" created upfront.

Nevertheless, warrants have genuine merits as an investment, primarily because they add LEVERAGE to an investment situation. This is a function of the fact that the price of a warrant always trades below the price of a share into which it converts, yet its price is inextricably linked to that share. As an example, take a company with shares which trade at 90p and warrants which trade at 20p. Assume also that the conversion price is 120p. Under these circumstances no one would convert their warrants. But if the share price doubled to 180p, the warrants would have INTRINSIC VALUE and conversion would be a sensible proposition. Now the warrants must trade at 60p minimum (share price less conversion price). For them to do less would mean that an opportunity for ARBITRAGE would be created. An investor could sell the shares, buy the warrants, convert and pocket the difference. However, in this scenario, although the share price has doubled, the warrant price has tripled. As always with leverage, the downside is magnified as well. So if the share price halved to 45p, the warrant price would fall much further. How much further would depend largely on how long there was to the warrant's expiry. For a short-dated warrant on a share with pretty glum prospects, the value would probably be little more than nominal.

Weight of money

A backstop explanation of why a stockmarket is moving upwards. If all else fails the "weight of money" argument is always worth a try because no one can disprove it and it has plausibility. Just as growth in an economy's money supply may well lead to higher prices for goods and services, it is reasonable to assume that extra money in the hands of big investors will lead to higher prices for stocks. Thus cash flows into and out of savings institutions are monitored by investment analysts as a factor that may influence prices.

Weighted average cost of capital

If a company is to succeed, in the long run its profits must exceed its cost of capital. Working out this cost means using the CAPITAL ASSET PRICING MODEL to calculate a DISCOUNT RATE for the cost of its EQUITY and taking the actual average interest rate on its debt. These two charges are then weighted according to the proportion of equity and debt in the total capital.

Wilshire 5000 Index

The most broadly based of all US COMMON STOCK price indices whose full name is now the Dow Jones Wilshire 5000. Despite its name, the index, which has a base date of December 31st 1980, comprises almost 4,600 stocks. Just over 80% of its value derives from stocks listed on the NEW YORK STOCK EXCHANGE, with almost all the balance coming from NASDAQ-listed stocks. It is weighted for the market value of its constituents, and at the end of 2008 it had a market value of $10.6 trillion.

Writer

The person who issues (writes) an OPTIONS contract and who assumes most of the RISK in much the same way as an insurance company in normal casualty business. Writers come in two forms:

- Covered, meaning that because of their own arrangements their risk, like that of the purchaser of the options contract, is limited.
- Naked, meaning that their potential LIABILITY is unlimited if things do not go the way they planned.

Someone who writes a CALL OPTION agrees to sell an amount of STOCK at a particular price within a specified period. In return he gets a fee upfront. He is betting that the price of the stock concerned will not rise much during the period in question. If he is right and he is covered (meaning here that he owns the stock in question), he will effectively improve his return on the stock. If he is wrong and the stock is "called away" from him, he will forgo extra profits as the stock's price continues to rise. Should he face an uncovered, or naked, call, his losses will be the difference between the market price of the stock to him less the PREMIUM he has received and the value of the contract's EXERCISE PRICE.

Writing a PUT OPTION means that the writer agrees to buy stock within the terms of the contract. He is betting that the stock's price will rise. If he is wrong, he will have to buy stock at above the market price and will face losses unless he has covered his position by SHORT SELLING the stock.

Yy

Yield

Generically, the return that someone gets from an investment, usually expressed as a percentage of the acquisition cost. Mostly, however, yield implies the return from income alone and, therefore, takes no account of changes in capital values (see TOTAL RETURN). In the case of a BOND, the yield usually refers to the so-called nominal yield, which is the bond's annual and fixed COUPON, or DIVIDEND, expressed as a percentage of the market price. In the case of an ORDINARY SHARE, the yield usually refers to the DIVIDEND YIELD, which is the latest full-year dividend paid on each of a company's shares as a percentage of the market price.

Yield curve

The graphical representation of the YIELD on bonds of increasing maturities. On the chart, time runs from left to right and yield is shown on the vertical axis. Thus, at a glance, investors can get an impression of the maturities where demand is strong and vice versa. Yield curves, which are used mainly for analysis of government BONDS, are put together by REGRESSION ANALYSIS of the various yields and maturities available. This is flawed to the extent that more information may be available for some maturities than for others. However, the overall picture can indicate which way investors expect interest rates to move.

Classically, the curve should slope upward as investors demand an increasing reward the longer they lend. A downward-sloping curve indicates that shorter-term interest rates are high and expected to fall. In practice, especially in the UK, the yield curve is "humped" in the range of seven- to ten-year maturities. This fits with the idea that short-dated government bonds are sought by banks for liquidity and regulatory requirements, while long-dated bonds are bought by pensions funds with liabilities stretching far into the future. In comparison, demand for medium-dated bonds is modest, hence the higher yields which the market demands to buy these securities. (See TERM STRUCTURE OF INTEREST RATES.)

Yield gap

A measure of the cheapness or expensiveness of EQUITIES versus government BONDS, expressed as the YIELD TO MATURITY on government bonds minus the DIVIDEND YIELD on ORDINARY SHARES. Other factors aside, the narrower the gap between the two, the cheaper the equities would be. For example, just before the stockmarket crash of October 1987, when (with the benefit of hindsight) equities were expensive, the yield gap in the United States was over seven percentage points. After share prices collapsed, and implicitly became cheap again, the gap narrowed to about four points.

It is nowadays the norm for bonds to yield more than equities. However, in the low-inflation 1950s when this benchmark started to be measured the opposite was often the case; risky shares yielded more than "safe" bonds. Thus the yield gap started life as share yields minus bond yields, so on rare occasions when bonds yielded more than equities the sum produced a minus figure, which was known as the "reverse yield gap". With the passage of time, the acceleration of inflation and a consistently higher yield on bonds, the sum was turned on its head and the expression "reverse yield gap" all but forgotten.

Yield spread

The difference in YIELD between BONDS of similar COUPON and TERM. Mostly this is a result of investors' qualitative assessment of respective borrowers: the Bundesbank will almost always be able to borrow more cheaply than the Bank of England; the US Treasury will borrow more cheaply than a top-quality corporation. Other factors also play a part: bonds with poor marketability will trade at higher yields than particularly liquid issues; if a government funds its debt heavily in a particular maturity range this will narrow the spread between itself and corporate borrowers.

Yield to maturity

Technically, the DISCOUNT RATE at which all outlays and receipts on a redeemable security net out at a present value of zero. Thus yield to maturity takes account of regular payments of income and capital gain or loss on redemption. Hence the term redemption yield in the UK. It is also the INTERNAL RATE OF RETURN. Take a BOND with five years to redemption standing at $123 in the market and paying semi-annual dividends of $6.50 for every $100 of nominal stock held (that is, $13 a year). Its running YIELD would be 10.6% ($13 as a percentage of $123). However, assuming the bond was repaid at $100, its yield to maturity would be only 7.4% to take account of the fact that the $23 of capital loss has to be written off over its remaining life.

Zero-coupon bond

An innovation of the early 1980s which can be useful for financial planning because it offers a lump-sum payment at a specified date in the future. Thus, for example, a company might issue zero-coupon bonds at $60 each with the promise that in seven years it will repay $100 for every $60 borrowed. Such a bond would have a YIELD TO MATURITY of virtually 7.5% per year; that is the compound rate at which value would accrue to the bond for it to reach $100 in seven years' time. Zeros have the added feature that they are particularly sensitive to changes in interest rates during their life, therefore they can be a good speculation for anyone betting on interest rates falling. However, in the United States the value that accrues to the bond each year is subject to tax, unless the bond is sheltered in a tax-free account.

In the UK, where zeros are most often issued as zero-dividend preference shares by investment trusts, big investors get the same tax treatment as in the United States. For private investors, though, the gains that accrue are still taxed as a capital gain on maturity, which is generally preferable to having them taxed annually against income.

Appendices

1 Stockmarket returns

UK

	Average growth (% per year)	*Standard deviation (%)*	*Compound growth (% per year)*	*Down years*
1918–25	12	24	9	2
1926–35	6	18	4	4
1936–45	2	12	1	4
1946–55	6	15	5	4
1956–65	7	21	5	6
1966–75	14	51	4	5
1976–85	17	15	16	1
1986–95	11	12	10	2
1996–2005	6	16	5	3
Total period	**9**	**25**	**6**	**31**

United States

	Average growth (% per year)	*Standard deviation (%)*	*Compound growth (% per year)*	*Down years*
1915–25	7	21	5	5
1926–35	6	36	–1	4
1936–45	5	19	3	4
1946–55	11	14	10	3
1956–65	8	15	7	3
1966–75	1	19	–1	4
1976–85	7	14	6	4
1986–95	13	12	13	1
1996–2005	9	16	8	4
Total period	**7**	**20**	**5**	**32**

Sources: UK index: BZW Equity index; US index: Dow Jones Industrial Average

2 Stockmarket performances

UK

Year end	FTSE-A All-Share[a]	Change (% per year)[b]	FTSE 100	Change (% per year)[b]
1968	174			
1969	147	-15		
1970	136	–7		
1971	193	42		
1972	218	13		
1973	150	–31		
1974	67	–55		
1975	158	136		
1976	152	–4		
1977	215	41		
1978	220	3	484	
1979	230	4	509	5
1980	292	27	647	27
1981	313	7	684	6
1982	382	22	834	22
1983	471	23	1,000	20
1984	593	26	1,232	23
1985	683	15	1,413	15
1986	836	22	1,679	19
1987	870	4	1,713	2
1988	927	6	1,793	5
1989	1,205	30	2,423	35
1990	1,032	–14	2,144	–12
1991	1,188	15	2,493	16
1992	1,364	15	2,847	14
1993	1,682	23	3,418	20

Year end	*FTSE-A All-Share*[a]	*Change (% per year)*[b]	*FTSE 100*	*Change (% per year)*[b]
1994	1,521	–10	3,066	–10
1995	1,803	19	3,689	20
1996	2,014	12	4,119	12
1997	2,411	20	5,136	25
1998	2,674	11	5,883	15
1999	3,242	21	6,930	18
2000	2,984	–8	6,223	–10
2001	2,524	–15	5,217	–16
2002	1,894	–25	3,940	–24
2003	2,207	17	4,477	14
2004	2,411	9	4,814	8
2005	2,847	18	5,619	17
2006	3,221	13	6,221	11
2007	3,287	2	6,457	4
2008	2,209	–33	4,434	–31
Compound growth (% per year)		7		8
Average change (% per year)		10		9
Standard deviation (% per year)		29		16

a "FTSE" is a registered trademark of the London Stock Exchange and the Financial Times Ltd and is used by FTSE International Ltd under licence.
b Capital value only.

United States[a]

Year end	*S&P 500 Index*[b]	*Change (% per year)*	*Dow Jones Ind Ave*	*Change (% per year)*	*NASDAQ 100*	*Change (% per year)*
1968	103.9		944			
1969	92.1	–11	800	–15		
1970	92.2	0	839	5		
1971	102.1	11	890	6		
1972	118.1	16	1,020	15		
1973	97.6	–17	848	–17		
1974	68.6	–30	616	–27		
1975	90.2	31	852	38		
1976	107.5	19	1,005	18		
1977	95.1	–12	831	–17		
1978	96.1	1	805	–3		
1979	107.9	12	839	4		
1980	135.8	26	964	15		
1981	122.6	–10	875	–9		
1982	140.6	15	1,047	20		
1983	164.9	17	1,259	20	133.1	
1984	167.2	1	1,212	–4	108.6	–18
1985	211.3	26	1,547	28	132.3	22
1986	242.2	15	1,896	23	141.4	7
1987	247.1	2	1,939	2	156.3	11
1988	277.7	12	2,169	12	177.4	13
1989	353.4	27	2,753	27	223.8	26
1990	330.2	–7	2,634	–4	199.4	–11
1991	417.1	26	3,169	20	326.7	64
1992	435.7	4	3,301	4	360.2	10
1993	466.5	7	3,754	14	398.3	11
1994	459.3	–2	3,834	2	404.3	2
1995	615.9	34	5,117	33	576.2	43
1996	740.7	20	6,448	26	821.4	43
1997	970.4	31	7,908	23	990.8	21
1998	1,229.2	27	9,181	16	1,836.0	85
1999	1,469.3	20	11,497	25	3,707.8	102

Year end	*S&P 500 Index*[b]	*Change (% per year)*	*Dow Jones Ind Ave*	*Change (% per year)*	*NASDAQ 100*	*Change (% per year)*
2000	1,320.3	–10	10,787	–6	2,341.7	–37
2001	1,148.1	–13	10,022	–7	1,577.1	–33
2002	879.8	–23	8,342	–17	984.4	–38
2003	1,111.9	26	10,454	25	1,467.9	49
2004	1,211.9	9	10,783	3	1,621.1	10
2005	1,248.3	3	10,718	–1	1,645.2	1
2006	1,418.3	14	12,463	16	1,756.9	7
2007	1,468.4	4	13,265	6	2,084.9	19
2008	903.3	–38	8,776	–34	1,211.7	–42
Compound growth (% per year)		6		6		9
Average change (% per year)		7		7		15
Standard deviation (% per year)		18		17		36

a Changes in capital value only.

b S&P 500 is a registered trademark of the McGraw-Hill Companies, Inc.

Japan			Hong Kong		
Year end	*Nikkei 225 Average*	*Change (% per year)*[a]	*Year end*	*Hang Seng Index*[b]	*Change (% per year)*[a]
1968	1,715		1968		
1969	2,359	38	1969	155	
1970	1,987	–16	1970	212	37
1971	2,714	37	1971	337	59
1972	5,208	92	1972	843	150
1973	4,307	–17	1973	434	–49
1974	3,817	–11	1974	171	–61
1975	4,359	14	1975	350	105
1976	4,988	14	1976	448	28
1977	4,866	–2	1977	404	–10
1978	6,002	23	1978	496	23
1979	6,570	9	1979	879	77
1980	7,063	8	1980	1,474	68
1981	7,682	9	1981	1,406	–5
1982	8,017	4	1982	784	–44
1983	9,894	23	1983	875	12
1984	11,543	17	1984	1,200	37
1985	13,083	13	1985	1,726	44
1986	18,821	44	1986	2,568	49
1987	21,564	15	1987	2,303	–10
1988	30,159	40	1988	2,687	17
1989	38,916	29	1989	2,837	6
1990	23,849	–39	1990	3,025	7
1991	22,984	–4	1991	4,297	42
1992	16,925	–26	1992	5,512	28
1993	17,417	3	1993	11,888	116
1994	19,723	13	1994	8,191	–31
1995	19,868	1	1995	10,073	23
1996	19,361	–3	1996	13,451	34
1997	15,259	–21	1997	10,723	–20
1998	13,842	–9	1998	10,049	–6
1999	18,934	37	1999	16,692	66

Japan			**Hong Kong**		
Year end	*Nikkei 225 Average*	*Change (% per year)*[a]	*Year end*	*Hang Seng Index*[b]	*Change (% per year)*[a]
2000	13,786	–27	2000	15,096	–10
2001	10,543	–24	2001	11,397	–25
2002	8,579	–19	2002	9,321	–18
2003	10,677	24	2003	12,576	35
2004	11,489	8	2004	14,230	13
2005	16,111	40	2005	14,876	5
2006	17,226	7	2006	19,965	34
2007	15,308	–11	2007	27,813	39
2008	8,860	–42	2008	14,387	–48
Compound growth (% per year)		4			12
Average change (% per year)		7			21
Standard deviation (% per year)		26			45

a Capital value only.

b Hang Seng Index is a registered trademark of HSI Securities Ltd.

Canada			**Germany**		
Year end	*S&P/TSX 60*[a]	*Change (% per year)*	*Year end*	*DAX Index*[b]	*Change (% per year)*
1968			1968	556	
1969	52.9		1969	622	12
1970	49.5	–6	1970	444	–29
1971	51.5	4	1971	474	7
1972	62.9	22	1972	536	13
1973	60.6	–4	1973	396	–26
1974	44.5	–27	1974	402	1
1975	48.9	10	1975	563	40
1976	50.8	4	1976	509	–10
1977	53.2	5	1977	549	8
1978	65.8	24	1978	575	5
1979	91.0	38	1979	498	–13
1980	113.9	25	1980	481	–3
1981	98.1	–14	1981	490	2
1982	99.7	2	1982	553	13
1983	127.2	28	1983	774	40
1984	120.4	–5	1984	821	6
1985	143.8	19	1985	1,366	66
1986	147.0	2	1986	1,432	5
1987	156.9	7	1987	1,000	–30
1988	167.5	7	1988	1,328	33
1989	198.0	18	1989	1,790	35
1990	168.4	–15	1990	1,398	–22
1991	184.4	9	1991	1,578	13
1992	175.1	–5	1992	1,545	–2
1993	221.5	27	1993	2,267	47
1994	221.8	0	1994	2,107	–7
1995	250.5	13	1995	2,254	7
1996	321.6	28	1996	2,889	28
1997	378.1	18	1997	4,250	47
1998	376.0	–1	1998	5,002	18
1999	495.9	32	1999	6,958	39

Canada			Germany		
Year end	*S&P/TSX 60*[a]	*Change (% per year)*	*Year end*	*DAX Index*[b]	*Change (% per year)*
2000	528.7	7	2000	6,434	–8
2001	442.6	–16	2001	5,160	–20
2002	373.2	–16	2002	2,893	–44
2003	458.7	23	2003	3,965	37
2004	511.9	12	2004	4,256	7
2005	634.7	24	2005	5,408	27
2006	742.8	17	2006	6,597	22
2007	808.5	9	2007	8,067	22
2008	541.8	–33	2008	4,810	–40
Compound growth (% per year)		6			6
Average change (% per year)		7			9
Standard deviation (% per year)		16			25

a Changes in capital value only. S&P/TSX 60 is a registered trade mark of the McGraw-Hill Companies Inc. and the Toronto Stock Exchange.
b Total return index.

Emerging markets			**France**		
Year end	*MSCI Emerging Markets*	*Change (% per year)*[a]	*Year end*	*CAC 40 Index*	*Change (% per year)*[a]
1987	100.0		1987	1,000	
1988	134.9	35	1988	1,580	58
1989	214.7	59	1989	2,001	27
1990	185.2	–14	1990	1,518	–24
1991	288.8	56	1991	1,766	16
1992	314.9	9	1992	1,858	5
1993	539.3	71	1993	2,268	22
1994	492.6	–9	1994	1,881	–17
1995	458.4	–7	1995	1,872	0
1996	476.3	4	1996	2,316	24
1997	412.5	–13	1997	2,999	30
1998	299.0	–28	1998	3,943	31
1999	489.4	64	1999	5,958	51
2000	333.8	–32	2000	5,926	–1
2001	317.4	–5	2001	4,625	–22
2002	292.1	–8	2002	3,064	–34
2003	442.8	52	2003	3,558	16
2004	542.2	22	2004	3,821	7
2005	706.5	30	2005	4,715	23
2006	912.7	29	2006	5,542	18
2007	1,245.6	36	2007	5,614	1
2008	567.0	–54	2008	3,218	–43
Compound growth (% per year)		9			6
Average change (% per year)		14			9
Standard deviation (% per year)		35			26

a Capital value only.

The World

Year end	*FTSE W World*	*Change (% per year)*[a]
1986	100.0	
1987	99.1	-1
1988	123.2	24
1989	151.3	23
1990	115.6	-24
1991	132.3	14
1992	127.4	-4
1993	149.9	18
1994	146.7	-2
1995	170.1	16
1996	194.2	14
1997	231.6	19
1998	272.7	18
1999	344.7	26
2000	314.0	-9
2001	267.2	-15
2002	201.6	-25
2003	247.9	23
2004	272.7	10
2005	312.8	15
2006	357.9	14
2007	374.4	5
2008	224.6	-40

Compound growth (% per year)	4
Average change (% per year)	5
Standard deviation (% per year)	18

a Capital value only.

3 Government bond returns and inflation

UK

Total returns, % per year

Year end	*Bonds*	*Inflation*	*Year end*	*Bonds*	*Inflation*
1981	4.57	11.88	1995	16.43	3.41
1982	41.72	8.60	1996	7.30	2.45
1983	13.61	4.61	1997	14.14	3.13
1984	8.87	4.97	1998	18.93	3.42
1985	12.01	6.08	1999	–0.92	1.56
1986	11.53	3.41	2000	8.75	2.93
1987	15.27	4.14	2001	3.04	1.82
1988	6.77	4.91	2002	9.25	1.63
1989	8.22	7.80	2003	1.70	2.91
1990	9.61	9.47	2004	6.94	2.96
1991	16.17	5.86	2005	9.45	2.83
1992	18.66	3.73	2006	–0.91	3.19
1993	21.01	1.57	2007	5.25	4.27
1994	–6.27	2.47	2008	12.01	3.99

United States

Total returns, % per year

Year end	*Bonds*	*Inflation*	*Year end*	*Bonds*	*Inflation*
1981	3.86	10.32	1995	17.42	2.83
1982	31.33	6.16	1996	2.91	2.93
1983	4.06	3.21	1997	10.00	2.34
1984	14.29	4.32	1998	10.25	1.62
1985	28.48	3.56	1999	–2.91	2.20
1986	21.03	1.86	2000	13.47	3.36
1987	–1.37	3.65	2001	6.69	2.83
1988	8.15	4.14	2002	11.48	1.59
1989	17.39	4.82	2003	2.25	2.27
1990	7.47	5.40	2004	3.48	2.68
1991	17.97	4.21	2005	2.74	3.39
1992	7.78	3.01	2006	3.09	3.23
1993	15.03	2.99	2007	9.05	2.85
1994	–2.90	2.56	2008	13.91	3.84

4 The world's leading equity markets, end-2008

Stock exchange	*Value*[a] *($bn)*	*Main index*	*Closing level*	*Market P/E ratio*	*Dividend yield (%)*
Australia					
Australian	693	S&P/All Ordinaries	3,659	11	6.5
Belgium					
Brussels	168[b]	BEL 20	1,909	5	11.4
Canada					
Toronto	1,033	S&P/TSX 60	542	10	3.6
China					
Shanghai	1,425	Shanghai Comp	1,821	10	2.8
France					
Paris	1,219[b]	CAC 40	3,218	8	5.4
Germany					
Deutsche	1,111	M-DAX	4,810	11	4.5
Hong Kong					
Hong Kong	1,329	Hang Seng	14,387	9	4.9
India					
National SE	600	S&P CNX 500	2,296	12	2.0
Italy					
Milan	522	S&P MIB	19,460	6	8.0
Japan					
Tokyo	3,116	Nikkei 225	8,860	10	2.7
Mexico					
Mexican	234	IPC Mexico	22,380	11	2.6
Netherlands					
Amsterdam	589[b]	AEX All-Share	381	5	7.7
Singapore					
Singapore	265	Straits Times	1,762	5	5.0
South Africa					
Johannesburg	483	FTSE/JSE All-Share	21,509	10	4.8

Stock exchange	*Value ($bn)*	*Main index*	*Closing level*	*Market P/E ratio*	*Dividend yield (%)*
South Korea					
KRX	471	KOSPI	1,124	8	2.7
Spain					
Madrid	948	Madrid SE	976	8	5.7
Sweden					
Stockholm	563[c]	OMX Stockholm AS	204	8	6.1
Switzerland					
SIX	880	SMI Index	5,535	13	3.1
Taiwan					
TWSE	357	TSEC Taiwan 50	3,329	9	8.2
UK					
London	1,868	FTSE All-Share	2,209	9	4.5
USA					
Nasdaq	2,396	Nasdaq Comp	1,577	...	...
New York	9,209	NYSE Comp	5,757	12	2.9

a Domestic companies only.
b Estimates based on value of Euronext.
c Includes all OMX Nordic exchanges.
Source: World Federation of Exchanges.

5 Investment formulas

Capital fulcrum point

CFP = [(e/(s – w))1/y] × 100%

Where:
e = exercise price
s = share price
w = warrant price
y = years to expiry of warrant

Black-Scholes model

Basic model for calculating the fair value of a call option on a non-dividend paying stock

Call price = S [N(d_1)] – E/ert[N(d_2)]

Where:
S = current stock price
N(d_1) = normal distribution function of d_1
E = exercise price of option
e = the base of natural logarithms (= 2.718)
r = risk-free interest at an annual rate
t = time to expiry of option (as a fraction of a year)
N(d_2) = normal distribution function of d_2

To solve for d_1:
d_1 = [ln(S/E) + (r + 0.5sd2)t] / [sd(t)1/2]
Where:
ln(S/E) = the natural log of S/E
sd = the standard deviation of annual returns on the share price (where the share price is squared, it is the variance)

To solve for d_2:
$d_2 = d1 - [sd(t)^{1/2}]$

Single index model

Shows a security's return as a function of the market's

$$R_{st} = a_s + b_s(R_{mt}) + e_{st}$$

Where:
R_{st} = the return on security $_s$ over period $_t$
a_s = the constant return on security $_s$
b_s = the sensitivity of the security's return to the market's return (ie, its beta)
R_{mt} = the market's return over period $_t$
e_{st} = the difference between the actual return on $_s$ during a given period and its expected return

Capital asset pricing model

$$E(R_s) = RF + \beta_s[E(R_m) - RF]$$

Where:
$E(R_s)$ = the expected return on security $_s$
RF = the risk-free rate of return
β_s = the beta of security $_s$
$E(R_m)$ = the expected return on the market

Capital market line

Shows the expected return from efficient portfolios

$$[E(R_m) - RF]/[sd(R_m)]$$

defines the slope of the market line, where:
$E(R_m)$ = the expected return from the market
RF = the risk-free rate of return

$sd(R_m)$ = the standard deviation of returns from the market

Thus the expected return from any portfolio on the capital market line is:

$E(R_p) = RF + \{[E(R_m) - RF]/[sd(R_m)]\}sd(R_p)$
Where:
$E(R_p)$ = the expected return on portfolio $_p$
$sd(R_p)$ = the standard deviation of returns on portfolio $_p$

Dividend discount model

Where the growth rate in dividends is assumed to be constant, the fair price of a common stock can be stated as follows:
$P = D/(k - g)$
Where:
P = the price of the stock
D = expected dividend
k = the required rate of return
g = the expected growth rate in dividends

From this, the required rate of return can stated as:

$k = (D/P) + g$

and the stock's price/earnings ratio as:

$P/E = (D/E) / (k - g)$

Where:
E = the expected level of earnings

6 Recommended reading

Highly recommended

Brealey, R. and Myers, S., *Principles of Corporate Finance*, 7th edn, McGraw-Hill, 2002.
Graham, B., *The Intelligent Investor* (4th edn), Harper & Row, 1973.
Greenwald, B. and Kahn, J., *Value Investing*, John Wiley & Sons, 2001.
Jones, C.P., *Investments Analysis and Management*, 6th edn, John Wiley & Sons, 1985.
Malkiel, B.G., *A Random Walk down Wall Street*, 6th edn, W.W. Norton, 1973.
"Adam Smith", *The Money Game*, Michael Joseph, 1968.
Train, J., *The Money Masters*, Harper & Row, 1980.

Others

Cottle, S., Murray, Roger F. and Block, F.E., *Graham and Dodd's Security Analysis*, 5th edn, McGraw-Hill, 1934.
Dreman, D., *Contrarian Investment Strategies*, Simon & Schuster, 1998.
El-Erian, M., *When Markets Collide*, McGraw-Hill, 2008.
Ellis, C.D., *The Investor's Anthology*, John Wiley & Sons, 1997.
Elton, E.J. and Gruber, M.J., *Modern Portfolio Theory and Investment Analysis*, 4th edn, John Wiley & Sons, 1981.
Galbraith, J.K., *The Great Crash*, Penguin Books, 1954.
Kolb, R.W., *Understanding Options*, John Wiley & Sons, 1995.
Lefevre, E., *Reminiscences of a Stock Operator*, John Wiley & Sons, 1993.

Lofthouse, S., *Equity Investment Management*, John Wiley & Sons, 1994.
McHattie, A., *The Investor's Guide to Warrants*, Pitman Publishing, 1992.
O'Shaughnessy, J.P., *What Works on Wall Street*, McGraw-Hill, 1998.
Roberts, R., *Wall Street*, Profile Books, 2002.
Smith, T., *Accounting for Growth*, Century Business, 1992.
Stewart, G.B., *The Quest for Value*, Harper Business, 1991.
Thaler, R.H. (ed.), *Advances in Behavioral Finance*, Russell Sage Foundation, 1993.
Train, J., *The New Money Masters*, Harper & Row, 1989.